BOARD N'STONES

TAKEMIYA MASAKI
COSMIC GO

BOARD N'STONES

『誰でもカンタン！図解で分かる囲碁AI流の打ち方』
Takemiya Masaki no uchuryu no gokui
by Takemiya Masaki
Copyright © 1993 Takemiya Masaki.
All rights reserved.

The German National Library lists this publication in the Deutsche National-
bibliografie; detailed bibliographic data are available in the Internet at
https://dnb.dnb.de.

ISBN 978-3-940563-93-4

© 2022, BOARD N'STONES, Gunnar Dickfeld, Frankfurt a.M.
BOARD N'STONES is a trademark of Brett und Stein Verlag

Cover design: Camille Lévêque
Translation: Malcolm Schonfield
Print: Books on Demand GmbH, Norderstedt

The Diagrams in this book were created with
SmartGo™: http://www.smartgo.com

Introduction

So far, I have gone through life making my own choices. I only have one life, and I want to live it without any needless restrictions. I want to continue moving forward in life, staying faithful to my true self.

We are all free, and this is a fundamental right; the very basis of our lives.

Go is like life. We are given a space where our freedom can express itself: the goban, with its three hundred and sixty-one intersections. However there is no point to this if we just play as others, or books, tell us to. Go is a world where you yourself are in control, and this is true whether you be a 1-dan, a 10-kyu, or even a beginner only just having learnt the rules.

You may agree or disagree with moves you have found in books, but simply reproducing them is absolutely pointless. Learning joseki by heart is also pointless. Imitating the moves of Meijin or Kisei title-holders is no better.

Even if you play well, you still should play as you feel. This is all-important. Otherwise the very act of playing go is, itself, pointless.

How can one learn to play good moves, moves that speak to one's heart?

Perhaps one way of progressing is to follow professional games. Try to look out for the good moves, even if you don't necessarily understand them. Contemplate these moves several times in your own home, calmly. You may not understand these moves at all, but that is not important. Your understanding of what is beautiful in go will develop, and this is very important.

A second requirement for playing well at go is to have a rich heart. This is very important, in fact it is indispensable.

One knows beauty when listening to sublime music. One may cry when watching a film. At these times your heart is speaking to you. This same full, rich heart is vital for making progress in go. You may think I am exaggerating, but read on: perhaps the game commentaries in this book will persuade you.

This book is based on go lessons I gave for two months on the NHK television channel. It is not a technical book; on the contrary, I continually stress the need to have a full heart, to dream... These are things you will not find in other go books.

Perhaps this will surprise some players, but I really do think that these subjects are important. They are certainly more important than the result of a game: it is a pity if you are overly sad because you have lost, or happy because you have won. These emotions will never help you progress.

We have discovered this extraordinary game called go. In the following pages, I hope to help you discover a new dimension to this world.

Takemiya Masaki

Table of content

Chapter 4: Problems   141

Chapter 1

The birth of the cosmic style

Often, players ask me: "How can I get better at go?"

This is all they want to know. I always answer: "You must place your moves wherever you wish, you must have a rich and generous heart, and you must look at the goban with clear eyes."

There is freedom in go. However, do you really play the moves that please you?

Are you perhaps afraid that people may make fun of you if you do not play according to the books? Such worries only put you under pressure and prevent you from playing good games.

The heart is the most important, in go as in life.

You have discovered this extraordinary game we call go. So enjoy it: play freely, and try to keep a pure and human heart when contemplating the goban.

Game 1: Win by fighting

Five-stone handicap game played in 1960 between
Takemiya Masaki, nine years old, Black, and
Tanaka Minaichi, then 5-dan, White.

"One should not try to make territory."
When I said this to an amateur who wanted to become strong, he just stared at me and laughed! His reaction is understandable. After all, go is a territorial game: if you have no territory, you can't win.

However, I ask you to remember above all that go is not just a territorial game. It is primarily a game of combat and balance.

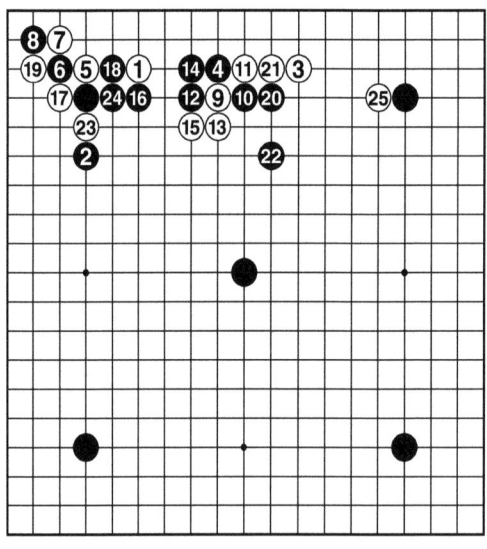

Figure 1 (1 – 25)

"Go is like life." I like to cite this phrase. Have you ever lost a game by trying to get too much money, i.e. territory, and by losing life, i.e. the shape of your stones?

Territory should be obtained naturally through the balance of the game and combat with the opponent. There will never be any beauty to your games if, right from the beginning, you think only of territory.

I feel a beauty in the shape of stones directed towards the centre. And I like the emotion beauty gives me.

People often call my style of play 'Takemiya's cosmic style'. But it's my natural style: I only play the moves that I like.

Maybe this introduction is too long. I would like to show you the first game I played against my mentor, Tanaka Manaichi, when I was nine years old. It is a memorable game, with a handicap of five stones. Between the ages of nine and thirteen, I played ninety games with Sensei Tanaka (professional 7-dan, now deceased). He had an enormous influence upon my style. He always told me: "Forget territory, win by fighting". He was displeased with me whenever I tried to make territory.

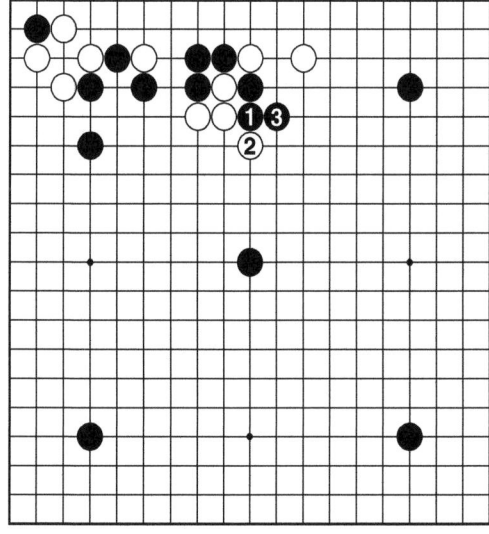

Dia. 1

Figure 1 – Diagram 1

When I was young, I was keen, but my style was crude. Everything is fine up till the bold invasion at 4. But because of Black's ignorance of tesuji, White makes profit up to 19. However, the nine-year-old boy that I was doesn't give up. He tries to fight back with 20, activating his stone 10.

We must note, however, that this move is not a tesuji. Despite the empty triangle they make, 1 and 3 in Diagram 1 are better.

Figure 2

It has been a long time since I last looked at this game, and I now find it horrible. It is full of ugly moves, and also directional errors. It would be more elegant for Black to play at A instead of 32, but this type of error isn't important. In this figure, the worst move is 34. Obviously, it should have been played at 37. What is most pressing at this point is the battle on the upper side. In this battle, Black clearly must reinforce the three cutting stones with 37.

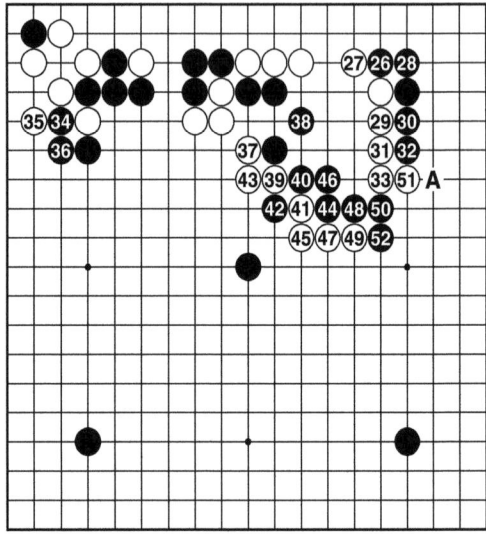

Figure 2 (26 – 52)

Amateurs often say: "I find it hard to read sequences correctly." However, I think that you don't have to read long sequences meticulously in order to play well. Perfect reading of long sequences is not so important. What is important is to 'feel' the moves. With intuition, one can sense the right shape of the stones, the flow of the game, and this is decisive.

It seems, though, that this nine-year-old boy just relied on his reading skills. Despite White's attack, with 37 at a vital point and the double hane of 39 and 41, he is able to save his group. But to do so, he has to play 48, a horrible move that makes an empty triangle. I still had a lot to learn.

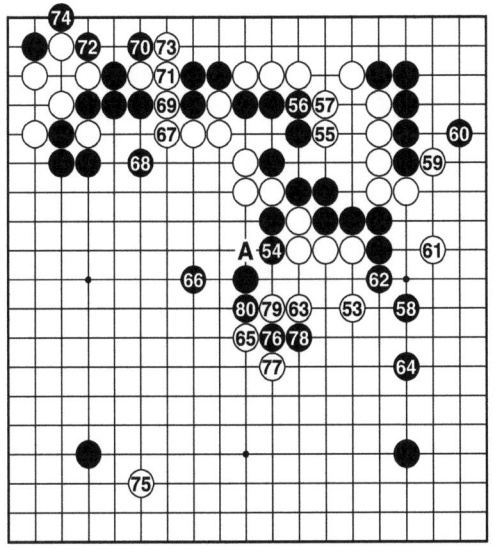

Figure 3 (53 – 80)

Figure 3

The boy that I was has a crude style. But, even so, we can see that he plays his moves as he feels them. White 53 is an overplay; the correct move would be A. Perhaps the Master wanted to test the child's strength.

Black 54 was surely played without hesitation. Sensei Tanaka said that it was a good move, and he rarely exaggerated. If we think that go is a territorial game, we may find other places more interesting to play in. But I like this move; it is looking for a fight. It does seem as if this boy has a very good global awareness. Thanks to 54, we can forgive him his mistakes.

Black 68 is a reading error. It is painful to let White capture three stones and thus save his group. However, it is not at all the same sort of mistake as Black 34.

Like 54, Black 76 was surely rapidly played. We feel the boy's vigour in this attack on White's central group. We ought to note, however, that 78 would be more severe at 79. Apparently, the boy was too vigorous and couldn't control himself.

Figure 4

Sensei liked to say to me: "In go, each player takes their turn to play, and plays only one stone at a time. In the final analysis, the value of a stone is the territory it serves to create. Therefore, in the middle of the game, it isn't at all worthwhile to play a stone just to make territory, or to take territory away from your opponent."

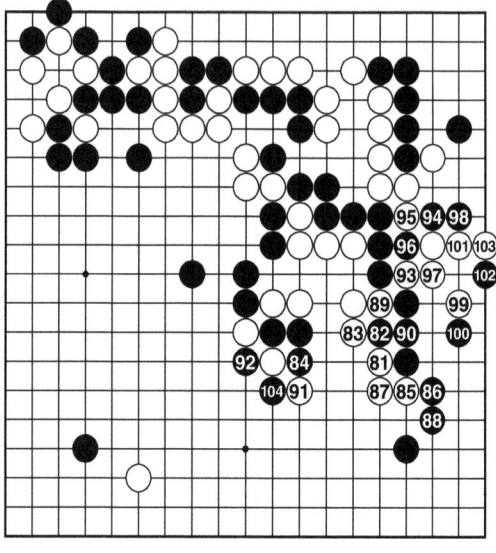

Figure 4 (81 – 104)

Although this is the first game played against Sensei, Black plays entirely as Sensei wishes: Black intends to win by provoking combat. However, as Black attacks violently, he leaves himself open to the elegant tesuji 85 and 87, and the Black group is caught after 93.

But does it really matter, that Black's attack failed? What would matter would be to forget the essentials – the shape of the stones and the direction of play.

Apparently, the boy couldn't read the semeai. After White 103, if Black plays at A, in Diagram 2, White captures five stones with B. If Black plays 1, White cuts at 2. In any case, Black cannot play A. After 6, if Black plays B, White plays C.

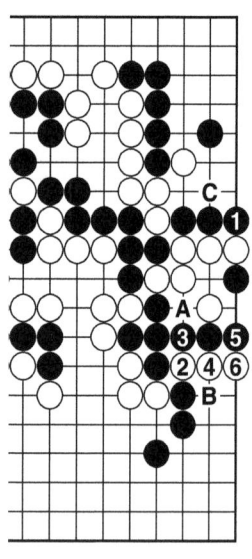

Dia. 2

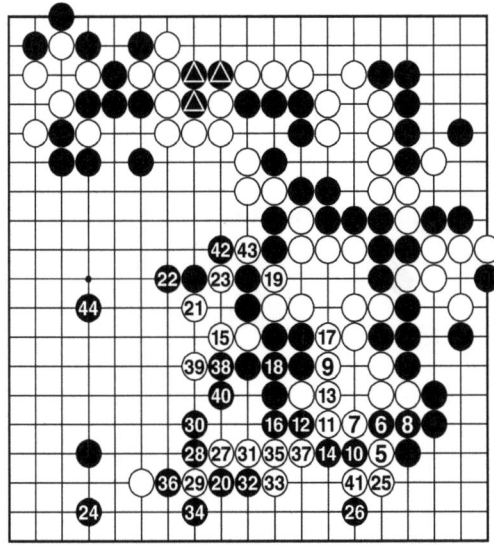

Figure 5 (5 – 44)

Figure 5

Black has lost the three ⬤ stones and his central group. But he still is lively and resists with hanekomi 6. Black 16 is far too slack. See Diagram 3 for the 'diabolical' move Black missed.

Black 22 is also a mistake. He hadn't seen the refutation, the tesuji 23 and 43. In spite of all this, Black still has the lead.

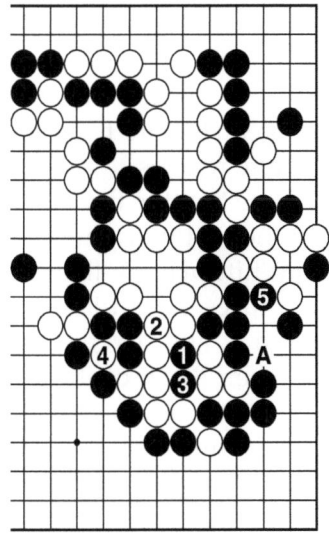

Dia. 3

Diagram 3

Had Black played horikomi at 1, he would have cried "Banzai!".

After Black 1, if White plays 3, Black gives atari at 2. So White has no choice and must play 2. Black next captures three stones, and can then capture the cutting stones with 5, as A no longer works for White.

It is a difficult tesuji, but this sort of move can be played by anybody who has studied tesuji. In go, 'feeling' is more important than reading. Start by learning about good shape.

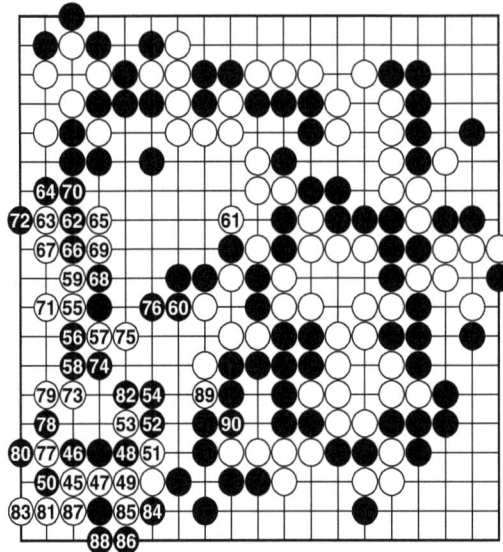

Figure 6 (45 – 90)

Figure 6

Happily for him, Black had a sente move at 60 on the left side.

This really is a violent game, but the fighting is without elegance, even if Black is apparently confident in his reading.

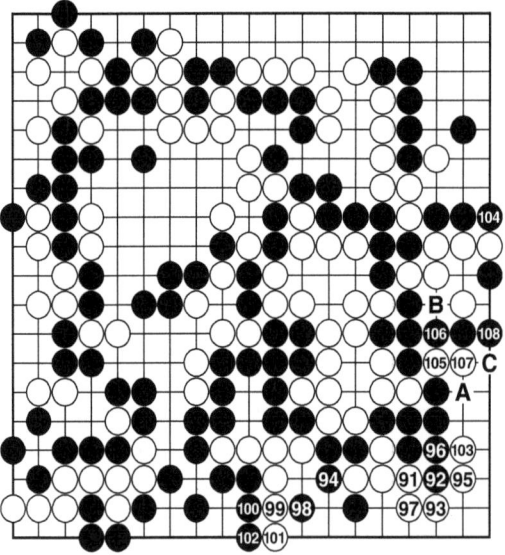

Figure 7 (91 – 108)

Figure 7

Black answers 91 and 93 with 94, and eventually succeeds in capturing seven stones. After 208 (noted 108 in the figure) White resigns.

Note that the Black group at the bottom right is alive: if White plays A, then Black captures the cutting stones with B, and if White plays C, then Black captures the three White stones with A.

This first game is made up of fighting and bad directional choices. Still, Sensei was satisfied with his pupil.

In all we played ninety games, the handicap going from five stones to one (i.e. sen). I won forty-three and lost thirty-seven games. Twice we had jigo, and six times we did not finish the game. Most of the games finished with a resignation, which shows that our games were combative.

Even now, Sensei's lesson 'Win by fighting' is the foundation of my style. Indeed, 'Takemiya's cosmic style', which doesn't aim primarily at making territory, results essentially from this lesson. Going back over this game played thirty years ago, I find that I already felt this very strongly. The child that I was then played according to how he felt, aiming towards combat. Perhaps my vision of the goban was more pure then than it is now.

Result: White resigns.

Game 2: At the beginning of the cosmic style

Even game played in 1969 between
Takemiya Masaki, then 5-dan, Black, and
Hashimoto Shoji 9-dan, White.

Instead of 'cosmic style', I prefer to use the term 'natural style'. I don't like to be enclosed, so naturally, my stones move towards the centre. Pay attention, and you may see a big central moyo appear. This often happens in my games.

Here I show you a game I played against Mr Hashimoto Shoji that shows the beginnings of the 'cosmic style'.

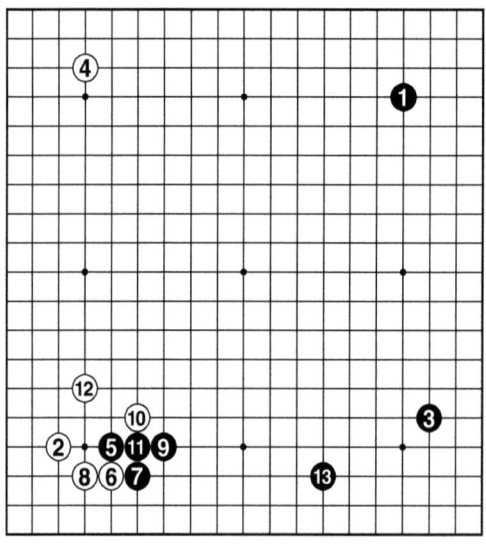

Figure 1

Black 13 is the move that I am proud of.

Figure 1 (1 – 13)

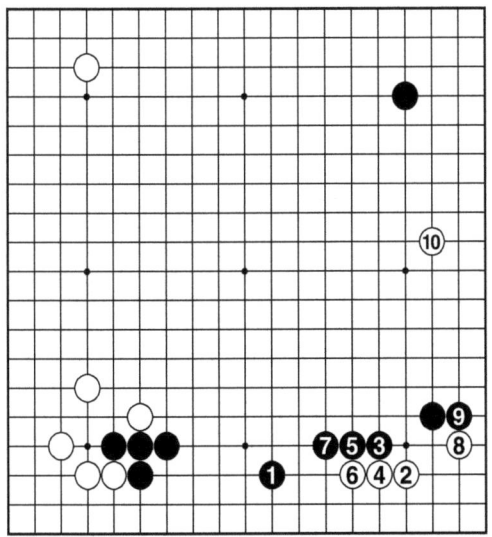

Dia. 1

Diagram 1

According to common sense (according to the joseki), one normally plays 1. But then, Black has no good answer to the kakari at 2. Even if he encloses White with 3 to 9, White still has a very good move: the wariuchi at 10.

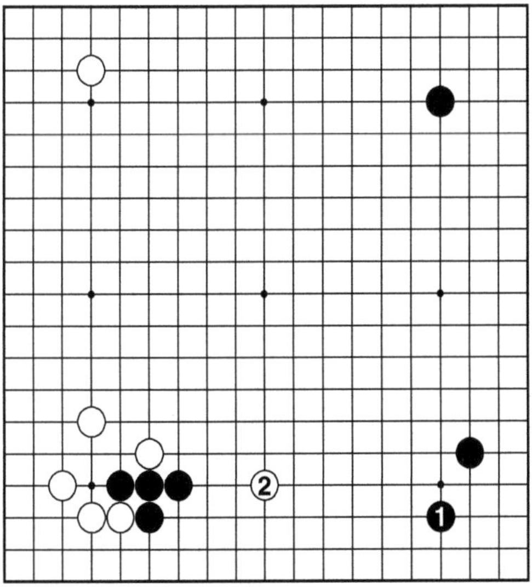

Dia. 2

Diagram 2

Making a shimari with 1 is another possibility.

However, White can attack the four stones on the bottom left with 2. One could try playing 1 at 5 in Diagram 1, but this seems too vague.

The idea of playing 13 comes from this analysis. What do you think of it? Although I'm proud of 13, I find that one can't 'read' a great deal from it.

Yes, but go is about 'feeling', not 'reading'.

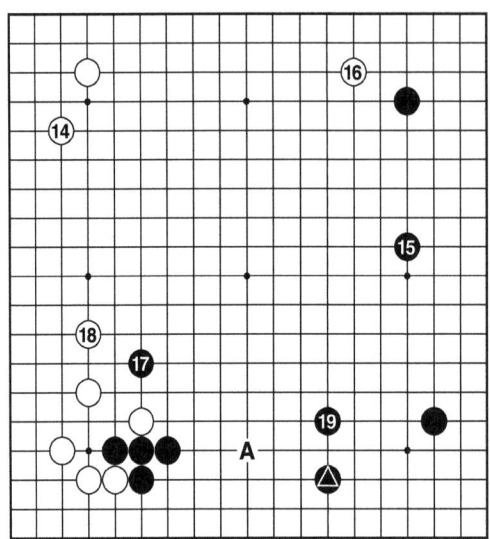

Figure 2 (14 – 19)

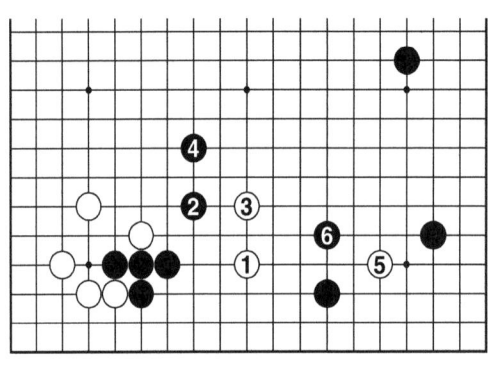

Dia. 3

Figure 2

One might be afraid of a white invasion at A, but Diagram 3 shows my plan to deal with that. In the game, up to 19, we see the creation of a big moyo stretching from the right to the lower side. To avoid this, White could have played 14 at 1 in Diagram 4. Also, 16 could have been played as in Diagram 5.

Diagram 3

If White invades with 1, then I am happy to escape towards the centre with 2 and 4. If White continues his attack with 5, then I separate his stones and attack both groups with 6.

What do you think of this plan? White is in difficulty, don't you think?

Because you are concerned about money (territory), you are afraid of the invasion at 1. It is true that in Diagram 3 White succeeds in invading the lower side; but only at the risk of his life (the shape of his stones). To have a worthwhile life (game), there must be something more important than money (territory). One shouldn't be preoccupied with immediate gain. In this, go and life are the same.

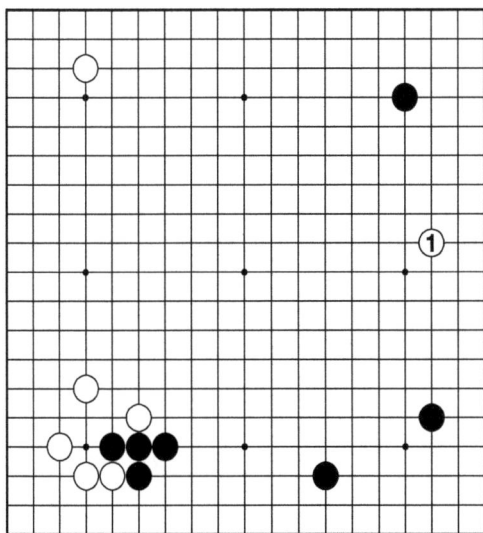

Dia. 4

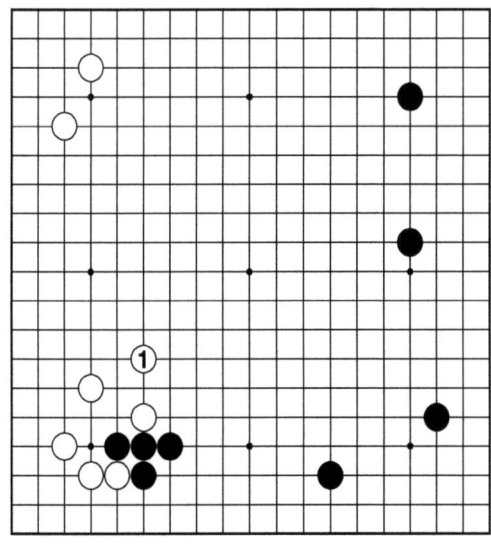

Dia. 5

Diagram 5

Playing White 16 like this is also possible. But in the game, White 14 and 16 are typical of Mr Hashimoto's very territorial style. In exchange, I obtain a large moyo.

Some people may wonder why Black didn't develop his moyo by playing 19 as in Diagram 6 (next page).

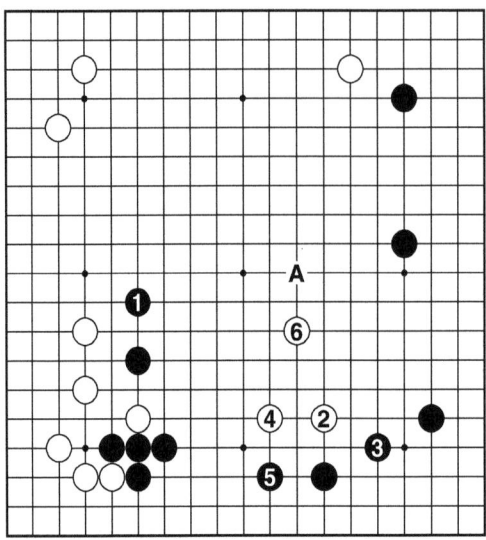

Dia. 6

Diagram 6

It is true that 1 is a very important point. But White will invade at 2. Black 3 follows and then White makes a good shape with 4 and 6. The question is: can White now be attacked? If you think you can attack with the cap (boshi) at A, go right ahead and try. Maybe you are more dynamic than I am. In go, you must play where you want.

It seemed to me that my moyo was large enough with 19.

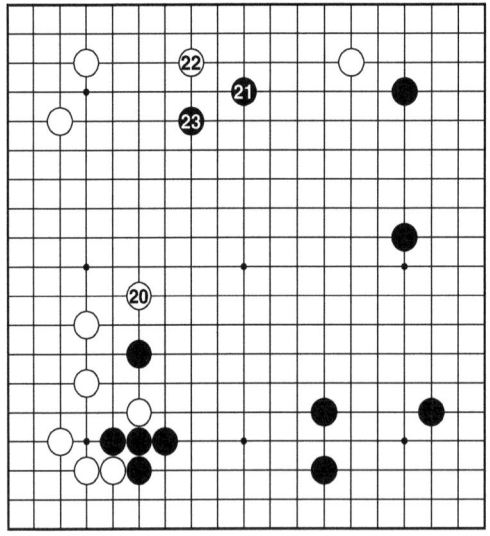

Figure 3 (20 – 23)

Figure 3

Now, White 20 is inevitable. I next pincered (hasami) at 21. What do you think of this move?

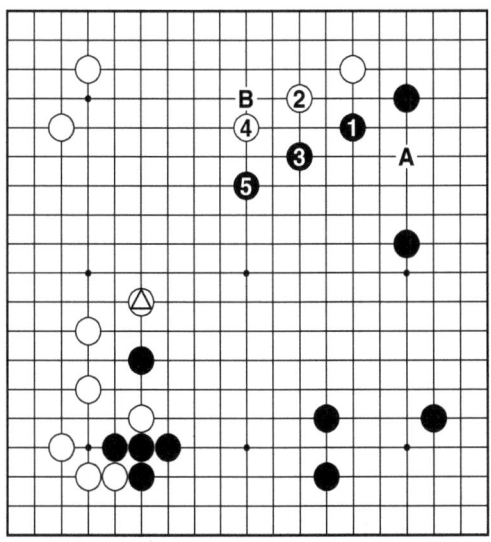

Dia. 7

Diagram 7

Those who think of playing the keima 1 instead of 21 have a good feel for the game. If White answers as shown, Black gets the upper hand in the centre. This is not bad at all.

However, those who thought of playing at A should watch out. White plays B and then the stone ⊘ becomes a magnificent move.

Again, the problem here is not one of reading, but one of 'feeling'.

In a certain sense, one can even say that go is simple. If you don't know what to play, then instead of trying to find the correct move, try to find the correct attitude. This will then lead you to a good move.

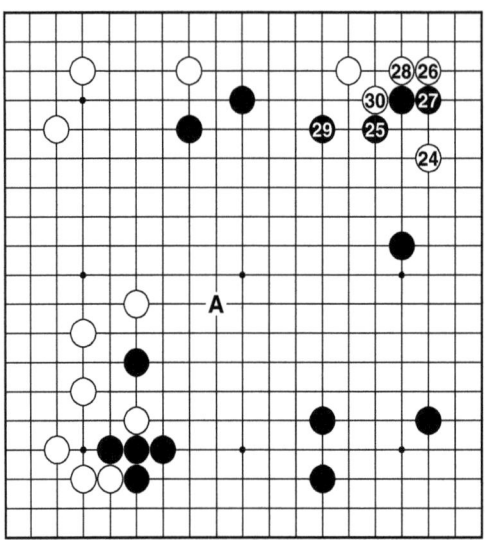

Dia. 2

Figure 4

I think it would surprise you to know that White 24 is a bad move, and makes White fall behind in the game. White should have played as in Diagram 8.

Diagram 9 shows a bad response to 24.

A good and simple answer to 24 is to play the kosumi at 25. White then occupies the san-san with 26, and then Black's moyo becomes firmer with 27 and 29.

White 30 is the losing move. It should be played somewhere in the region of A, to reduce the moyo.

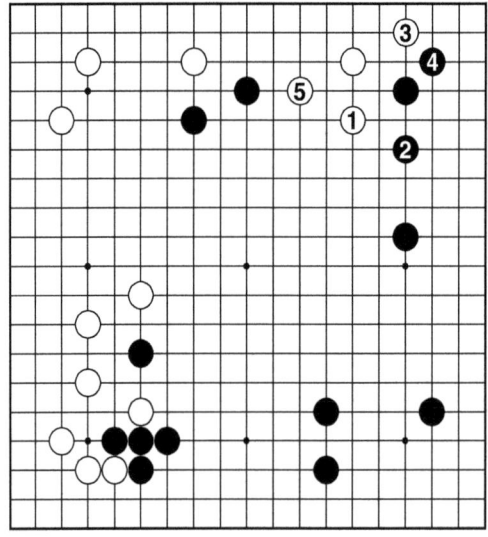

Dia. 8

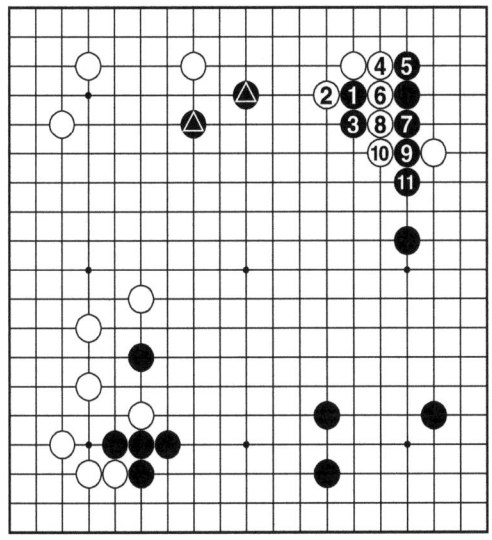

Dia. 9

Diagram 9

In response to 24, Black 1 and 3 do not work very well. White can follow the sequence up to 10.

According to reference books on joseki, Black then gets a better result. People who think so, in this case, are hard workers. Unfortunately for them, they place undue reliance on their knowledge, and lack global sense.

Although Black does make a lot of territory with the sequence up to 11, the two ▲ stones will be attacked, and the big black moyo easily erased, which is enough for White. You shouldn't believe everything you read in books! They only contain general indications. As two board positions are never the same, we must all find the right moves for ourselves. It is ridiculous just to learn joseki by heart.

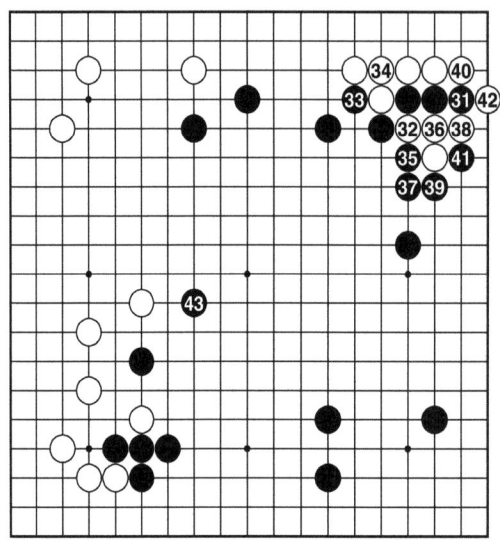

Figure 5

The sagari at 31 is the decisive move. It is a sacrifice; White captures the three stones, but then Black takes the key point with 43. The game is almost wrapped up.

Figure 5 (31 – 43)

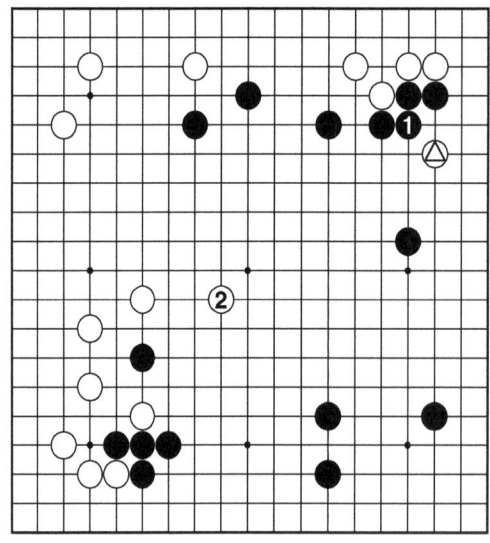

Diagram 10

If one does not want to sacrifice the stones, one can connect with 1 – but there is no beauty to this shape. Not only is there still some life to the ⬡ stone, but above all, I am unhappy that White gets to play first in the centre with 2.

Dia. 10

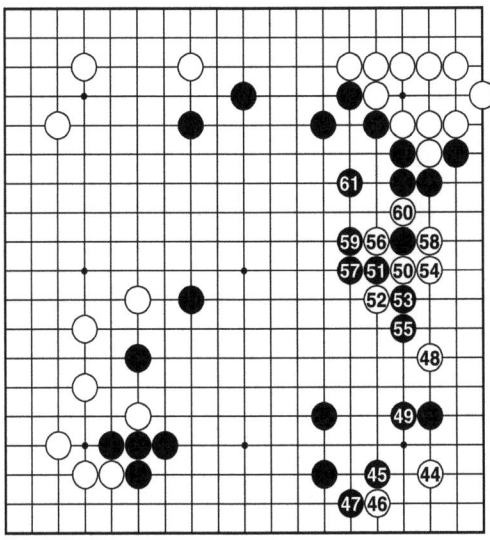

Figure 6　(44 – 61)

Figure 6

Move 44 is a yosu-miru, aiming at turning the tables on Black. Black just answers simply at 45. He does not have to look for complications. When White tries to live in Black's moyo with 50 and 52, Black does not even have to kill. Black just has to confine White to the edge, and let him live on a small scale.

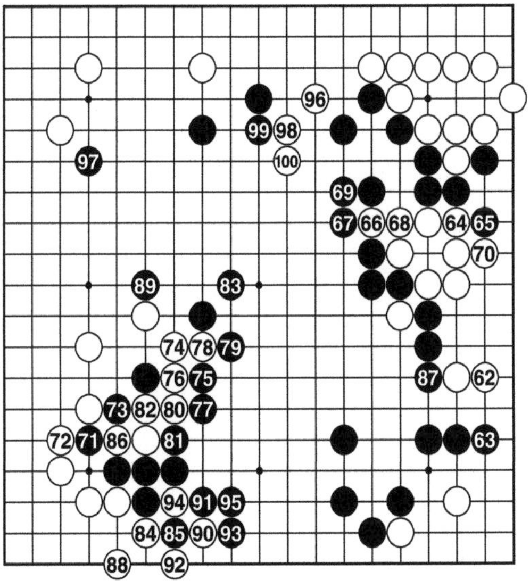

Figure 7

Now we clearly see that the central black moyo has become territory.

Figure 7　(62 – 100)

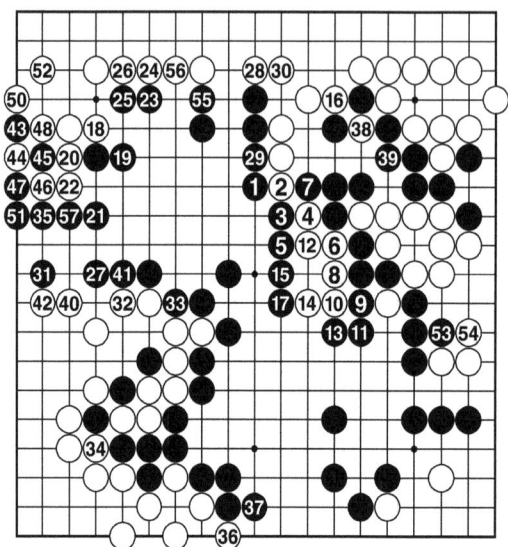

Figure 8 (1 – 57)

49 connects (at 44)

Result: White resigns after 157.

Figure 8

The immense territory that Black has built in the centre is now worth over one hundred points. White is now very much behind in the game, and resigns after 157.

To each their own. Some like to make territories here and there and play solidly. Others only think of winning. In my case, the goban is the place where I express my dreams...

Game 3: The art of attacking

Game played in 1974 between
Takemiya Masaki 7-dan, Black, and
Kato Masao 8-dan, White.

Usually if you make a moyo, your opponent will invade it. You then need to be strong at attacking. However, many players have misunderstood what attacking means. They confuse 'attacking' with 'killing' and try at all costs to capture and kill the opponent's stones. If they fail, then all is over – a sad end to a game, don't you think?

Don't mix up 'attacking' and 'killing': learn the art of attacking.

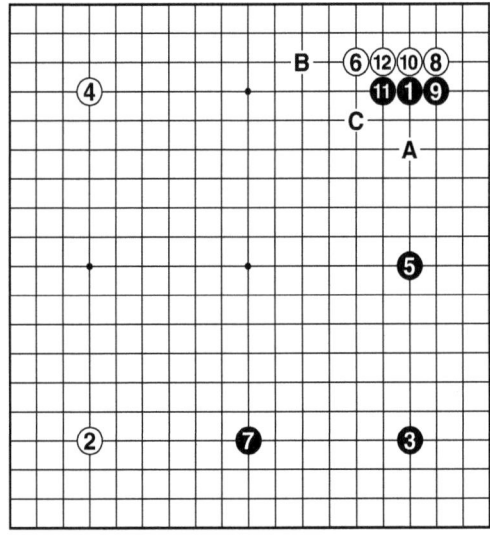

Figure 1 (1 – 12)

Figure 1

After White's kakari at 6, Black plays tenuki and takes the big point at 7. There are other possibilities for 7: you can answer the kakari at A, or pincer at B, or build a moyo with C…

Once again, I say to you: you can play wherever you want to in go. Even so, you must not choose the wrong direction. For example, playing 9 at 10 would be a bad choice of direction. Do you understand why?

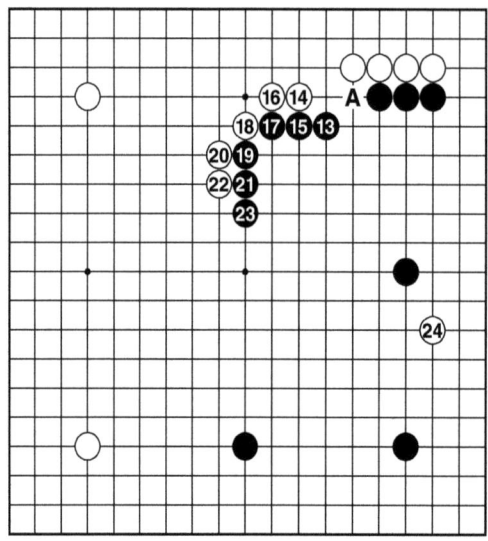

Figure 2 (13 – 24)

Figure 2 — Diagram 1

Move 13 is very important. Such key moves, or tennôzan[1], often appear at the beginning of moyo games. Move 13 is a good example of a tennôzan. If Black plays 13 elsewhere and White turns at A, it is almost certain that Black will lose the game. Move 13 is vital.

In answer to White 14 and 16, Black 15 and 17 are also very important. White's double hane 18–20 is the most severe tesuji. But Black must not give way. Up to 23, each move is extremely important. Perhaps some players may ask themselves why I insist so much on these moves. It is because, in a moyo game, the boundary between the two moyos is the most important factor. For instance, if Black plays as in Diagram 1, White pushes up immediately at 2. As you can see, the black moyo then does not function at all.

When White invades at 24, Black has a chance to attack!

---

[1] *Here Takemiya uses the term 'tennôzan'. This military term means 'the key to victory', and comes from a fable of two warring lords. The victor was the one that first occupied the mountain called 'tennôzan'. (Translator's note)*

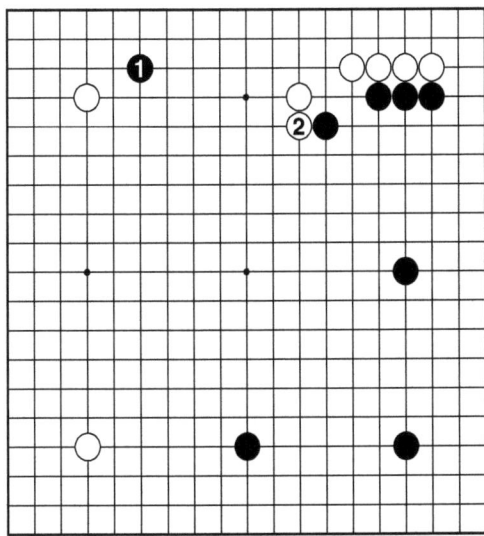

Dia. 1

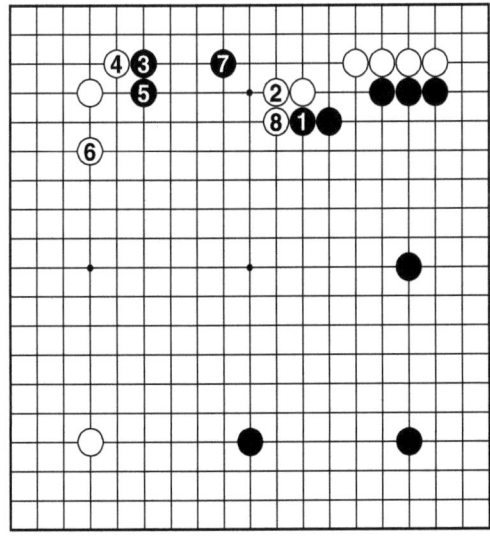

Dia. 2

Diagram 2

Some players push only once at 1 (after move 13 in the game) and then play the kakari 3. Is this because 1 is a kikashi? Or because Black was able to play on both sides? What rubbish! Black's sanrensei loses all of its value because of the excellent White magari at 8. Also, the three black stones on the top side are weak. If you tend to play like this, I recommend that you avoid choosing the sanrensei.

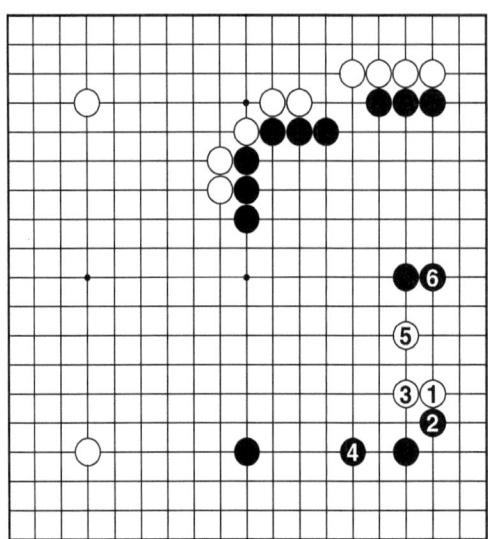

Dia. 3

Diagram 3

If White invades with the kakari 1, what should Black do? This situation is often written about in books, so I am sure you will find the solution. Yes, Black plays the tsuke at 2 to take away White's eye space, and follows up with 4. Next, after 5, Black plays solidly at 6. In fact, 6 is a good move not because it makes territory, but because it attacks the White group.

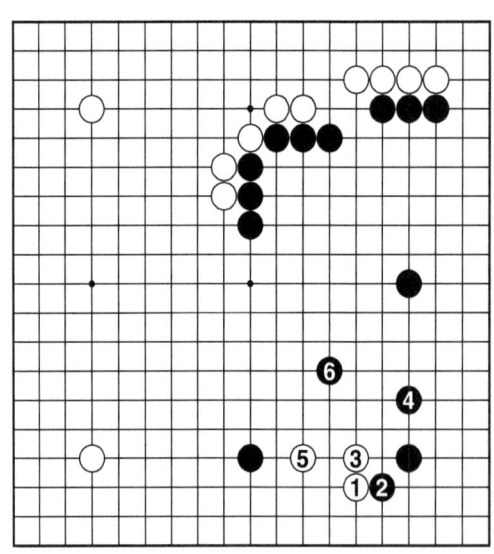

Dia. 4

Diagram 4

If White approaches from the other direction, Black still plays 2 and 4, but after 5, it is more interesting to attack with 6 and develop the moyo at the same time.

I haven't calculated everything, but intuitively I prefer 6.

Let's go back to the game.

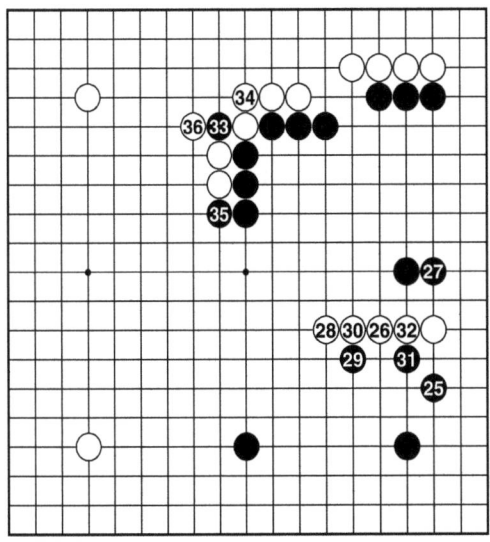

Figure 3 (25 – 36)

Figure 3

I chose to attack with 25. White plays a tobi at 26 and Black stops White settling with 27. Black plays two nozoki at 29 and 31, then plays 35, a very important move. Black has really hit his stride.

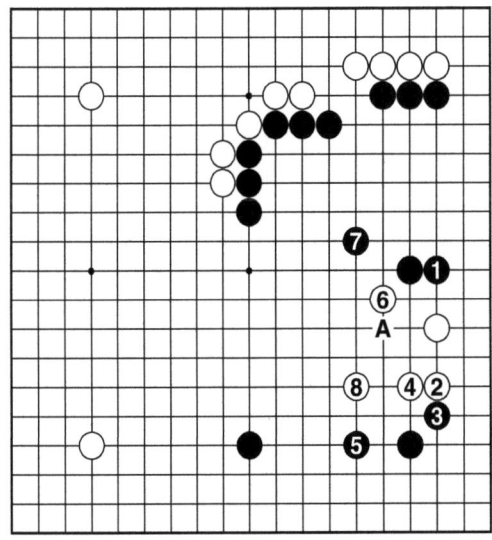

Dia. 5

Diagram 5

Black 1 is also possible. If White plays 2 at A, then Black plays at 2. This is 25 and 27 played in a different order.

After 8, I feel that the white group is under less pressure than in the game, which is why I chose not to play this sequence.

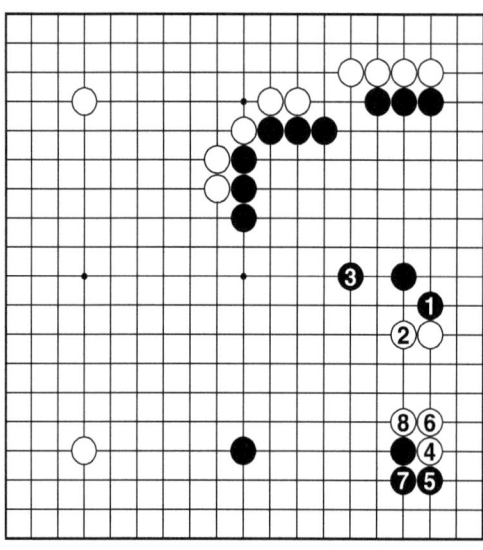

Dia. 6

Diagram 6

Black 1 and 3 are also possible, but I do not like these moves. Compared with the other Diagram, I feel that Black is being greedy, and is just aiming for territory.

Black 1 and 3 are not even very pretty. White stabilises his group with 4 to 8. This is not very good for Black.

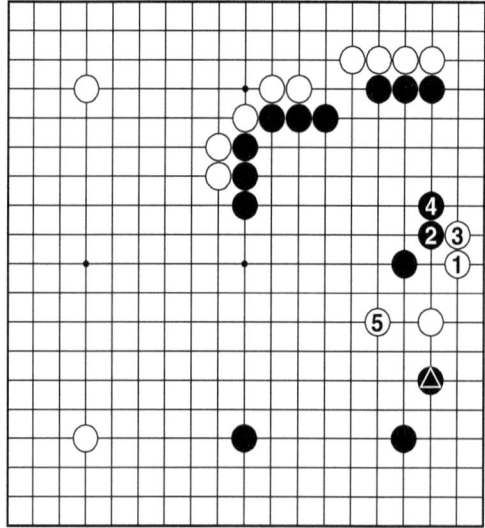

Dia. 7

Diagram 7

I played ⬤ for all these reasons. If you don't play here, it's probably because you don't want White to play the suberi 1. After 2, White plays a kikashi at 3 and the tobi 5. This is bad for Black. The problem is Black 2. It looks normal but is in fact a bad move.

This move shows that Black is too concerned with making territory!

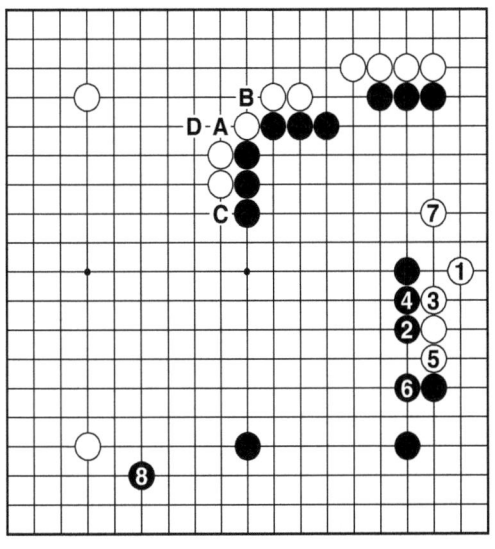

Dia. 8

Diagram 8

The correct answer to White 1 is the tsuke 2. White then invades the whole side with 3 to 7.

Is this such a bad result for Black? People who say so believe that the sides are the most important thing in go. White does succeed in invading the right side, but Black's kakari at 8, together with the influence given by the two stones 2 and 4, create a big moyo for Black. Once again, it's a question of the centre.

As in the game, Black has many kikashi on the top side (for example, as in the game, Black A, White B, Black C and White D). Black's central strength is therefore very important. Look at the goban more globally: if you only think of the little island (Japan), you'll never get out into the rest of the world...[1]

---

[1] *Takemiya is referring to the Japanese, with a good dose of humour and irony (Translator's note).*

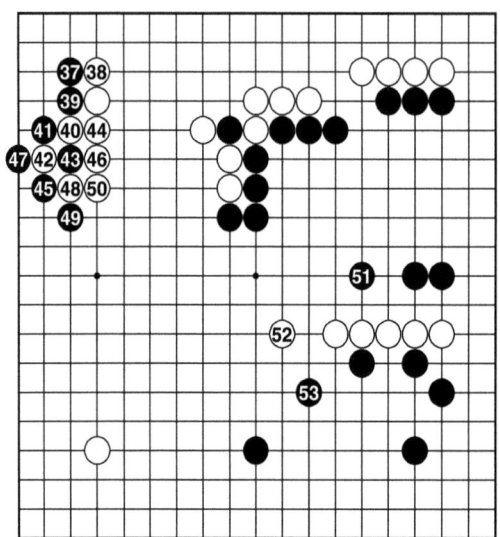

Figure 4 (37 – 53)

Figure 4

Instead of pursuing the attack, Black invades at the san-san (a big point). Then Black keeps up the pressure with the tobi 51.

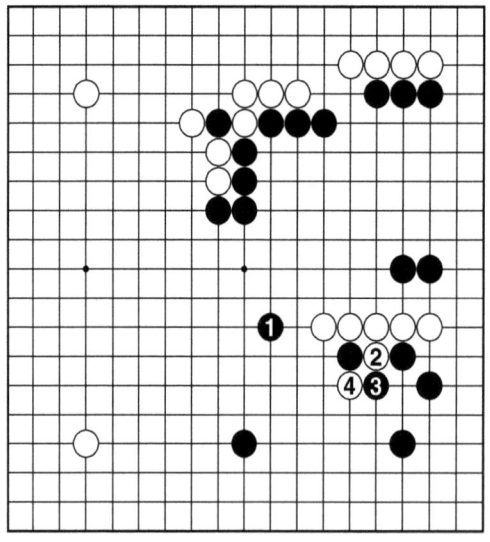

Dia. 9

Diagram 9

Of course, Black could directly attack with the capping move (boshi) at 1, but will this attack work? One must be flexible in go. Some people think that they can't win unless they kill invading stones. But go is not as simple as that.

White flees with 52 and Black follows with a keima at 53. What do you think of this attack? Is it too peaceful and easygoing?

Black makes territory while attacking, and lets White run away. This is the correct sanrensei strategy.

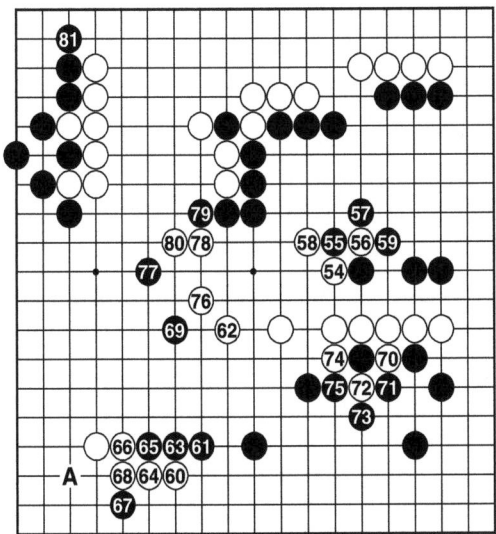

Figure 5 (54 – 81)

Figure 5

Let's look at how the game continued. With 54 to 58, White tries hard to get back into the game, but Black keeps up his attack from afar with 61. This attack continues right up to move 80.

During this, Black takes points on all sides. In the bottom left corner, the san-san at A is still open. After 81, Black has a big lead.

White was able to invade and escape, but this did not cost Black any territory. Do you see? I told you at the beginning of this game that 'attacking' and 'killing' are two different things. I hope that you understand this now.

Result: White resigns.

Game 4: An enormous moyo

Even game played in 1974 between
Takemiya Masaki 8-dan, Black, and
Ishida Yoshio, Honinbo, White.

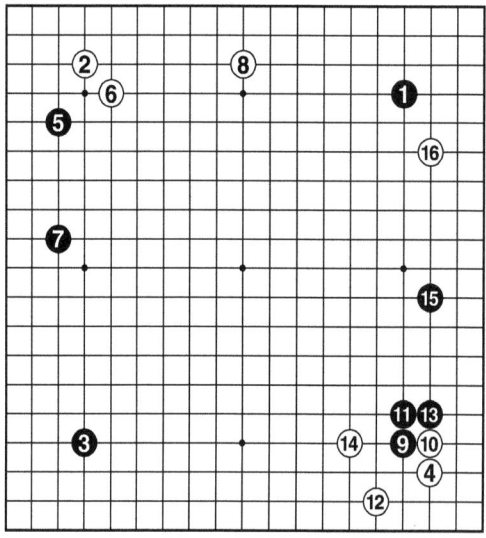

Figure 1 (1 – 16)

Mr Ishida has a territorial style. So against him, I always end up making a big moyo. This suits me perfectly; perhaps it suits him as well.

Figure 1

White 6 and 8 are good examples of Mr Ishida's style. He plays calmly at the beginning, and often wins his games thanks to his precise calculations.

For Black 9, there are other possibilities (see Diagram 1).

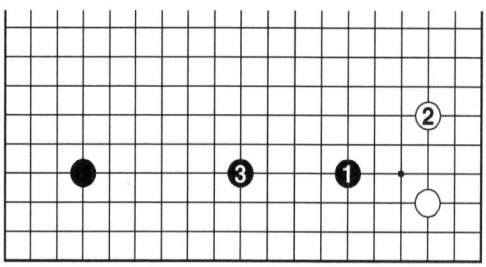

Dia. 1

Diagram 1

Developing the lower side with 1 and 3 is also possible.

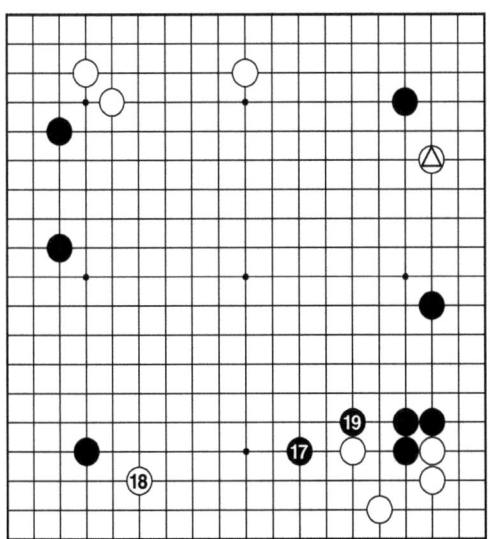

Figure 2   (17 – 19)

Figure 2

Instead of responding to the kakari ⊘, I played at 17. Then, once again, I played the tsuke at 19 instead of answering the kakari at 18. I was aiming for the centre.

I am probably the only go player who would play in this way (see Diagram 2 for the usual continuation). I also have some remarks to make about move 18 (Diagrams 3 and 4).

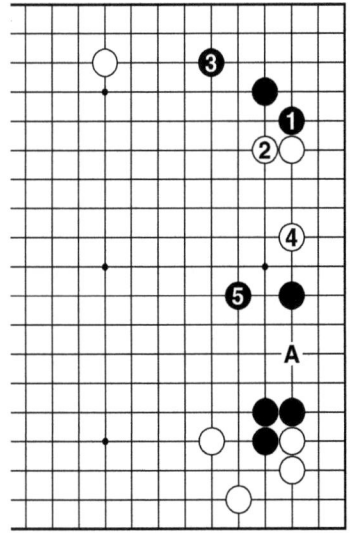

Dia. 2

Diagram 2

Instead of Black 17, many players would think of the sequence 1, 3 and probably 5 (tenuki instead of 5 would be dangerous because of the invasion at A). There is nothing wrong in choosing this sequence, but it gives another game. No one can say if 17 and 19 are really correct or not. I just judged that these two moves would not put me behind.

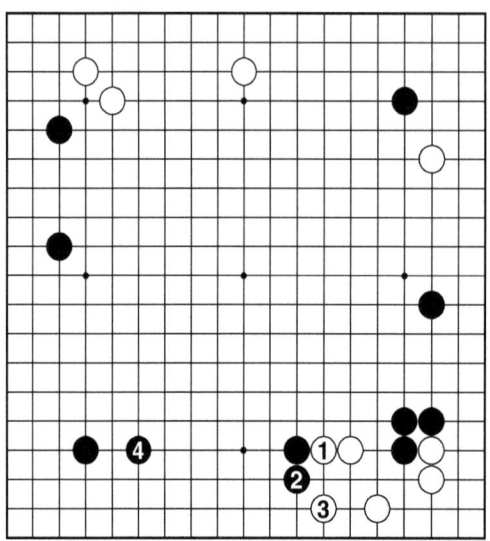

Dia. 3

Diagram 3

To avoid being enclosed, White must play 1 and 3. But Black can then make a shimari with 4, and this is enough for Black.

Suddenly, a large moyo is born, around the lower and left side.

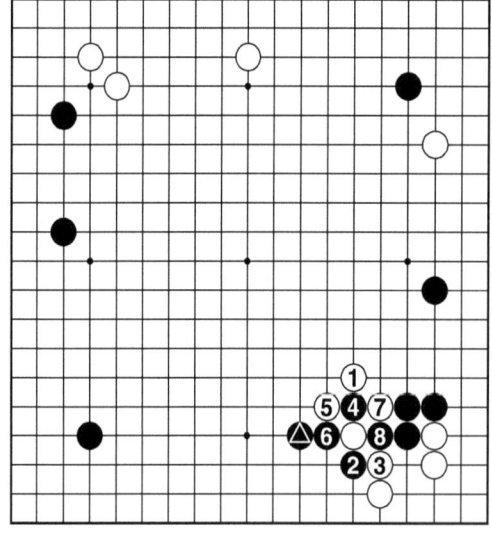

Dia. 4

Diagram 4

The white tobi at 1 gives Black a lot of aji to play with later on. For instance, the tesuji 2 and 4 cut off the stone 1 from the rest of the group.

One of the reasons for playing ⬤ is that it leaves no good move for White in this area.

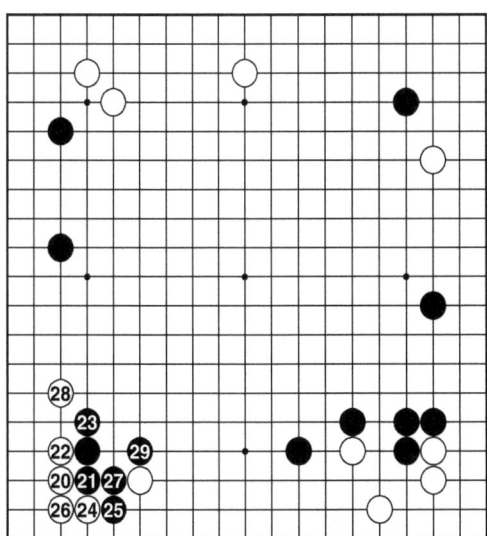

Figure 3 (20 – 29)

Figure 3

After the kakari at 18, White takes the san-san with 20; Mr Ishida does like a territorial strategy.

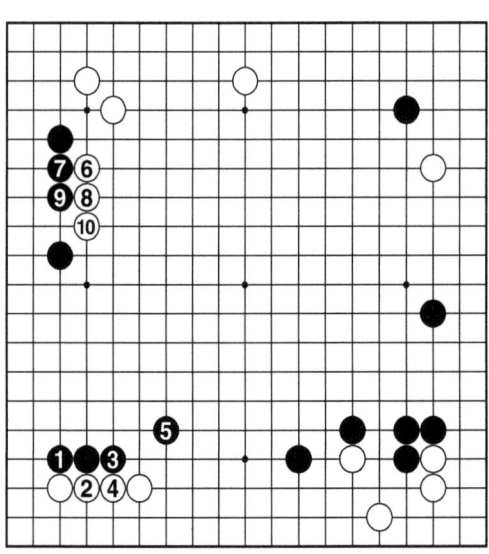

Dia. 5

Diagram 5

Instead of 21, some players would undoubtedly play 1. But then, White can play 6.

In fact, these ideas don't come from my reading, they come from my intuition.

The difficulty of moyo games is that the wrong choice of direction makes one immediately fall behind.

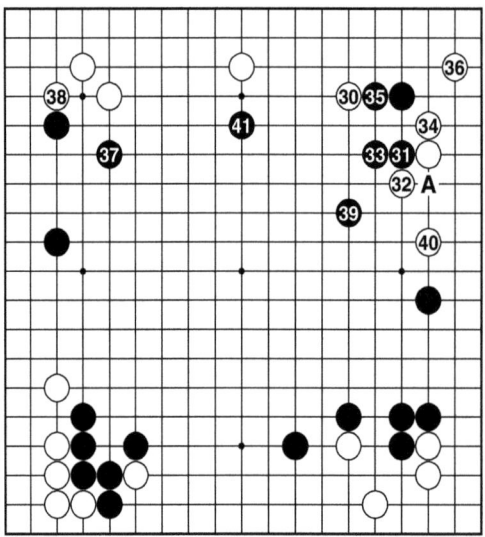

Figure 4 (30 – 41)

Figure 4

After the second kakari at 30, it is natural to move out towards the centre with 31 and 33. This sort of move can never be bad.

After the two exchanges of 37–38 and 39–40 (there is a cut at A if White plays tenuki after 39), Black makes an enormous moyo with the boshi at 41.

This has to be one of the most dynamic games I have ever played; at this point of the game, I felt fine.

I have a few remarks to make about Black 31 and 33.

Diagram 6

Many players would play as in this Diagram, but this is a bad idea. When White encloses the Black group with 6, the two stones ⬣ no longer have any meaning. Trust influence. If you decide to make a moyo, you must not stay in the corner.

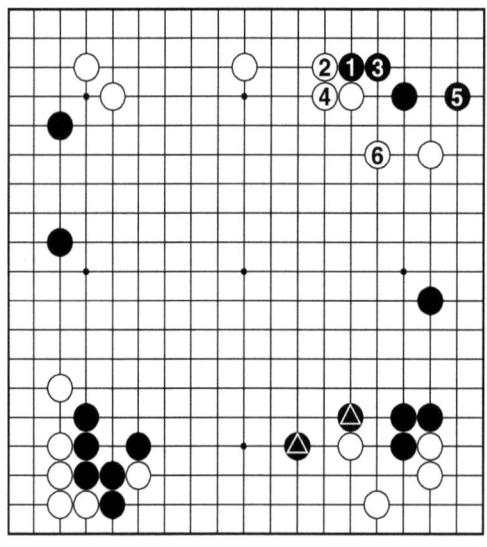

Dia. 6

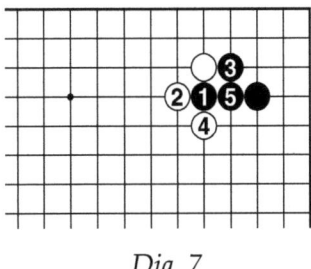

Dia. 7

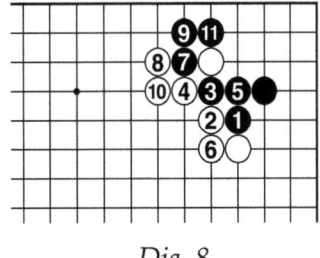

Dia. 8

Diagrams 7 and 8

By the way, I would like to show you some joseki that I do not like at all. In particular, we have the joseki in Diagram 7. This joseki is in fashion at the moment, but robs the hoshi of all its value, which is why I do not think much of it.

The joseki in Diagram 8 is one way of avoiding the taisha. But can a move that creates such a bad shape be any good? I find that stones are beautiful when they are directed towards the centre.

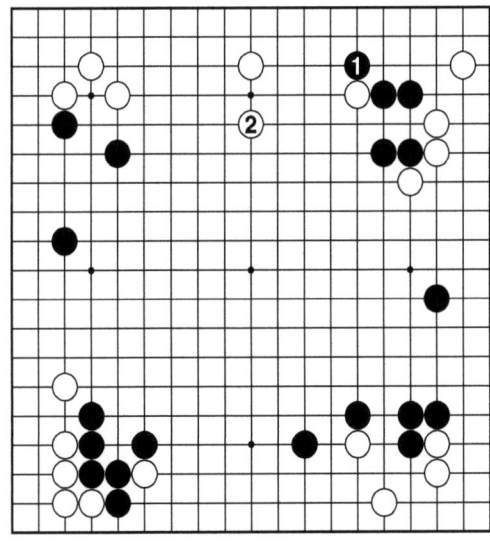

Dia. 9

Diagram 9

Black 1 is said to be joseki. But in this game, White 2 becomes a superb move. Black 1 is a fine example of a move that is locally good, but globally extremely bad.

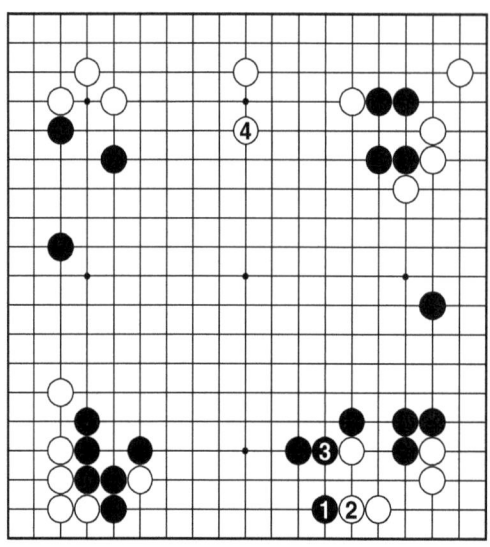

Dia. 10

Diagram 10

Reinforcing the lower side with 1 and 3 gives a similar result: White will play 4.

One can see that this point (at White 4) is un-doubtedly the vital point of the game.

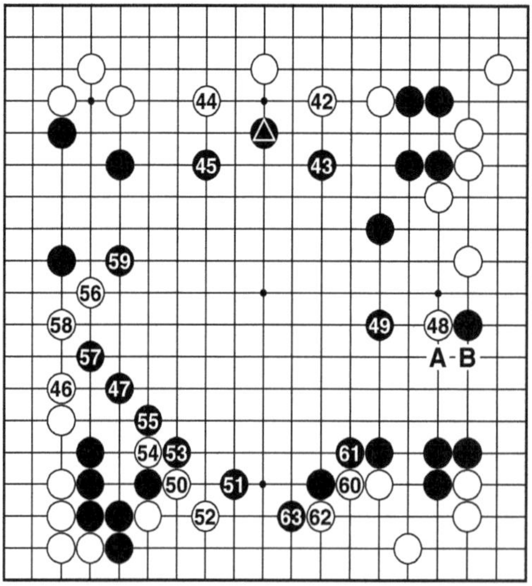

Figure 5 (42 – 63)

Figure 5

With the boshi at ⚫, Black has the lead. White 42 and 44 are necessary, but Black easily blocks White and reinforces his moyo up to 45.

Note Black's reply at 49 to the tsuke at 48. According to 'common sense', Black would normally either hane with A, or nobi at B. What's most important here, however, is the battle for the centre.

Black 57 and 59 prevent White from gaining access to the centre. Up to 63, Black succeeds in creating a large moyo (which is not territory). Black is clearly in the lead.

However, I made some mistakes later on in the game, and in the end I lost.

Despite this, and for many reasons, for me this is a memorable game.

Result: Black resigns.

Game 5: An 'abnormal' 5–5 move

Even game, played in 1978 between
Takemiya Masaki 9-dan, Black, and
Fujisawa Hosai 9-dan, White.

Often, I tend to forget things. I am not at all proud of this. For instance, I forget appointments. The worst is when I forget the game I played the day before.

However, a poor memory is not necessarily a bad thing for a go player. Players are often habitually dependent on their past games. When they are in a complicated position, they say to themselves: "I've played the same kind of game before; how did I deal with the situation then?"

Luckily or not, as I completely forget the past, I can always look at the goban with a certain freshness. 'Common sense', theory, habit... How we are dependent on these things without even knowing!

Think about it: two games are never identical in go. So what is written in books, or what commentators say, is nothing more than a question of 'common sense'. In go, one must think for oneself. I am against depending on 'common sense'.

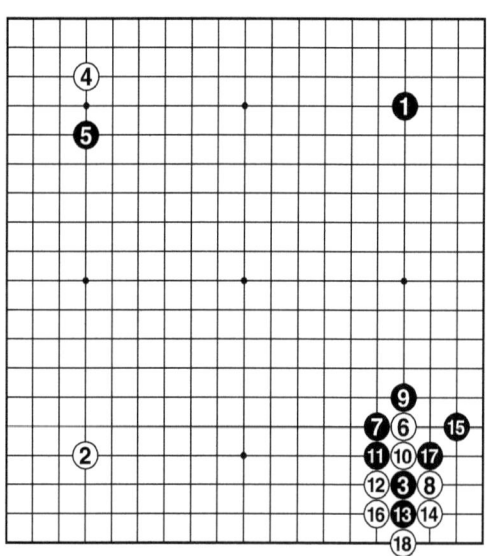

Figure 1   (1 – 18)

Now, I would like to show you a game that completely goes beyond 'common sense' [1]. Of course, the theme of the game is the centre, in particuliar with a move at the 5-5 point.

Figure 1

In response to Black 7, White 8 is Sensei Hosai's favourite joseki. He must have been attracted by the corner territory. But I'm also happy as I gain influence.

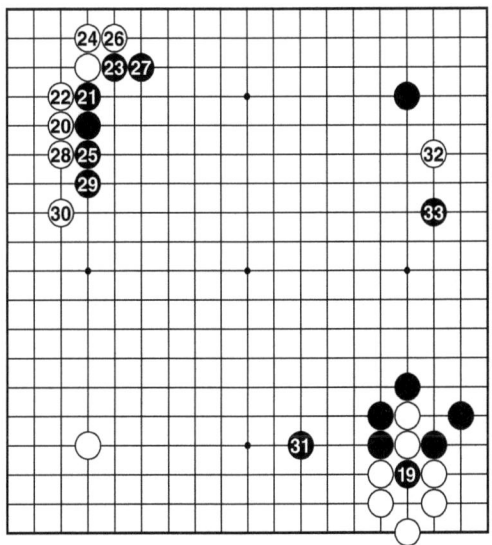

Figure 2   (19 – 33)

Figure 2

Black can play 21 at 28; but here, I feel that my choice of 21 is more in line with the spirit of this game.

Up to 33, each player pursues his plan: White plays in a territorial manner and Black aims at the centre.

---

[1] *The term 'common sense' is widely used in Japan. It often refers to social norms, describing how people are supposed to behave. (Translator's note)*

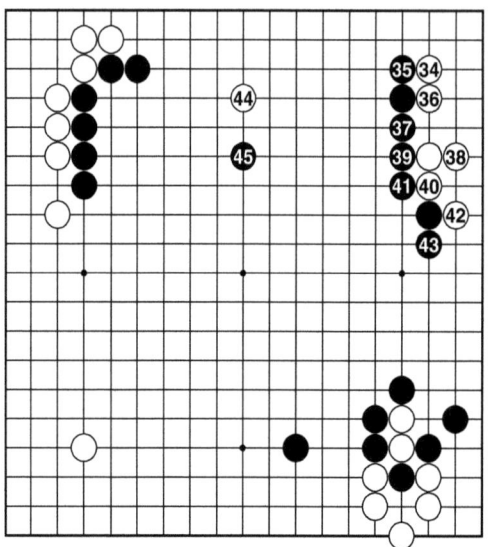

Figure 3 (34 – 45)

Figure 3

Perhaps one might tell me that 35 is abnormal: "If there isn't a black stone somewhere around the point at 44, then 35 is not a good move."

Everyone, or at least dan-ranked players, knows this theory.

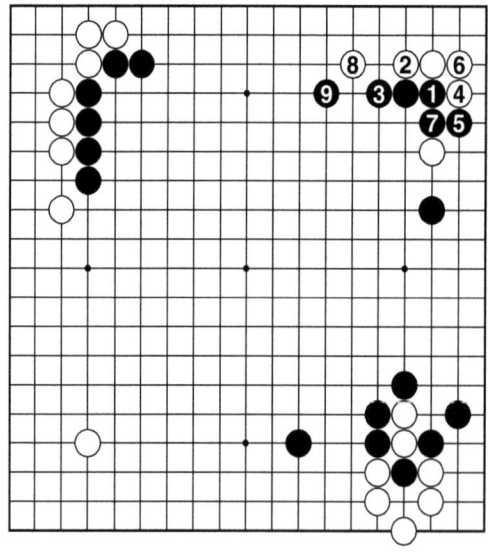

Dia. 1

Diagram 1

Normally, Black plays 1. After 8, Black reinforces the moyo with 9. Black gets a lot of influence on the right side, which is not bad at all. Even so, I was so keen to play 35 that I just went right ahead and did it.

Back to the game: White's invasion at 44 is necessary. With the cap (boshi) at 45, I make a big moyo in the centre instead of along the right side (see also Diagram 2).

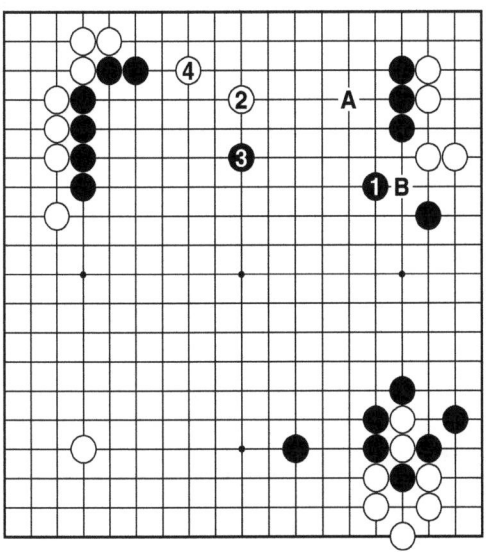

Dia. 2

Diagram 2

The keima 1 is the joseki move. As in the game, let us suppose that White invades with 2, and that 3 and 4 follow. I find that this variation gives Black more weaknesses (for instance, White can play A or B).

From the moment one decides to take the centre, one should be more concerned with influence, or thickness, than with territory. In the game, although 39 loses a few points compared with 1 in this Diagram, it is more solid.

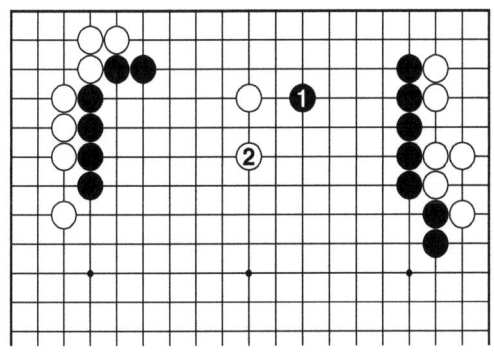

Dia. 3

Diagram 3

Some might prefer to play 1 so as to make territory, but this is no good at all, because of White's tobi at 2. The black stones' light, shining towards the centre, is reduced to nothing by this move.

In a difficult situation, instead of asking yourself how you should play, you can ask yourself in what spirit you should play.

Here, the centre is vital to Black. If you understand this, you cannot even begin to imagine Black 1. It is obviously played in the wrong direction.

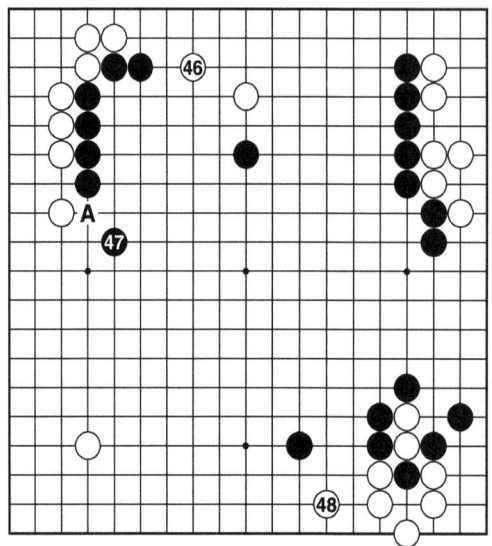

Figure 4 (46 – 48)

Figure 4

Black 47 is also an important move for this central strategy. Playing 47 at 48 is a very tempting alternative, but I was afraid that White would ruin my central strategy by answering at A.

Now, try to imagine the next move. One can't find this move by relying entirely on 'common sense'.

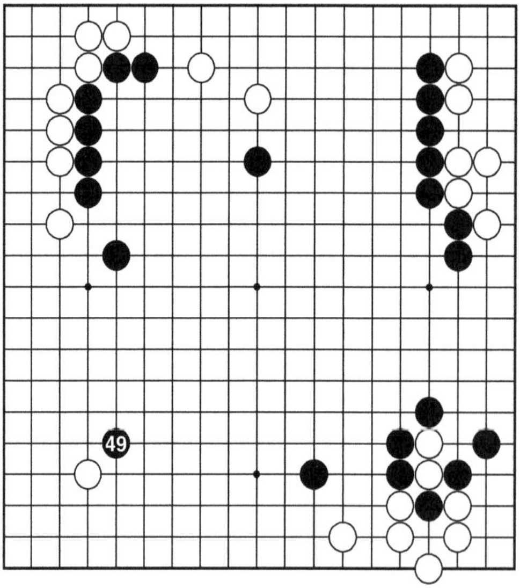

Figure 5 (49)

Figure 5

I played 49 at the 5–5 point. You will never find this move in a joseki dictionary. Still, I believe that this is the best move to express my ambitions for the centre.

One is free in go. Instead of depending on the past, it is essential in go to depend only on yourself, and to think for yourself.

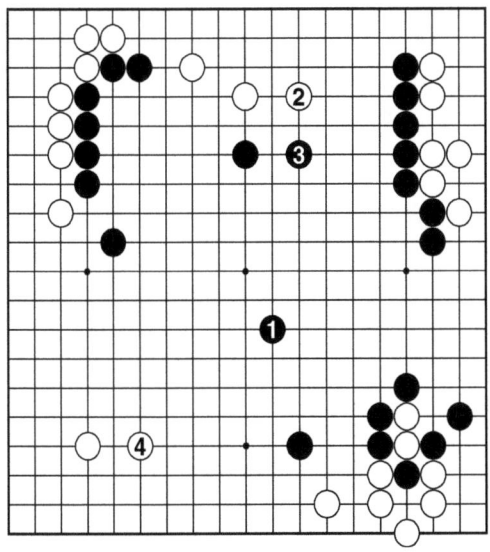

Dia. 4

Diagram 4

Black does have ways of making territory. But to actually do so with 1 is the worst choice. White plays kikashi at 2, and then makes a shimari with 4.

By the way, Black 1 is a good example of a purely territorial move.

Figure 6 (50 – 70)

Figure 6

Undoubtedly, White should have played 52 at 54, as Black gets an extremely solid central force up to 57. Also, for players worried about territory, Black still has the san-san at 65 in the bottom left corner. So we see that the 5–5 move was not bad at all.

Even so, it is true that Black has lost all four corners. I probably have the most experience among all professional players of games where one player loses all four corners.

An old go proverb says: "If you lose all four corners, resign," but I say the opposite: "If you can't accept losing all four corners, don't play go."

The game is very difficult because of the resolute invasion at 58. But I felt fine at this point. White's territory in the corners is not all that big. On the other hand, all the black stones are shining and participate in the central battle. I could never felt uneasy in such a situation.

Black does not have to capture the 'invader' in order to win. As he can attack both the white group on the upper side and the white stone in the centre, Black is sure to make profit.

Once again, the direction of the attack is all-important.

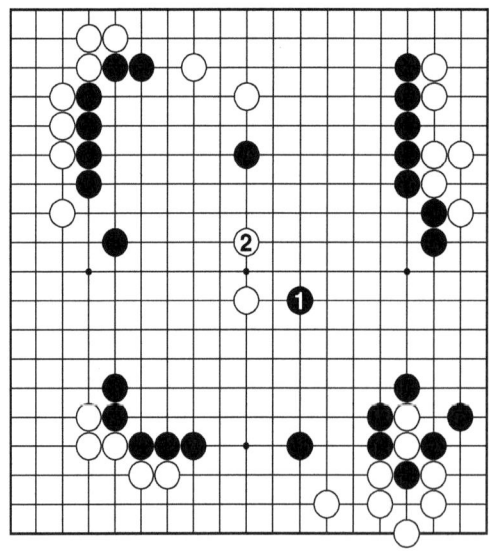

Dia. 5

Diagram 5

This attack, motivated by making territory on the right side, is not good. With 2, White easily makes sabaki.

The correct attack is 59 in the figure. This move also reinforces the weak stone marked ▲ in the figure; it is the right direction.

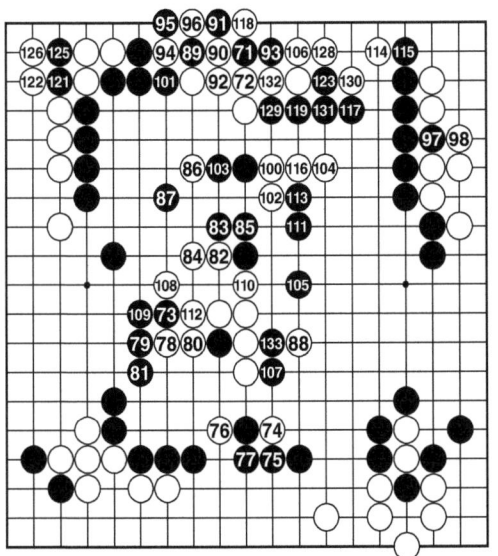

Figure 7 (71 – 133)

99 at 89, 120 at 96,

124 at 94 and 127 at 89.

Figure 7

Here is the rest of the game. I give no detailed commentary here. If one is able to play up to this stage of the game, then winning or losing becomes less important. If Black attacks well, he wins. If not, he loses. It is the process that is important.

The result of a game (a win or a loss) is little compared with the beauty of go. Our duty, as professionals, is to give you fine games, for your instruction and pleasure.

My message is simple: do not be bound by 'common sense' or theory; play the moves that please you.

Result: White resigns.

Chapter 2

The sanrensei in the cosmic style

The term 'cosmic style' often refers to my use of the sanrensei. The sanrensei is ideal for enclosing enemy stones while keeping positions high and favouring influence. I have developed the use of the sanrensei since it fits well with the way I 'feel' go.

Some players may say: "If you always play the same way, your opponents can prepare their strategy to counter your sanrensei."

I simply answer: "Is go so small that my opponent can make me lose just by preparing a strategy?"

No, go is not so limited. It has immense potential; there are countless variations that rest largely unexplored. While my opponents search to find ways of countering the sanrensei, I try to invent original variations and new developments.

Instead of asking such sterile questions, play the moves that you really want to and try to get to grips with the meaning behind these moves.

The sanrensei is in fashion but many play it without even understanding its meaning. It aims for central influence, and gives rapid development. By playing at the hoshi in the corner, one takes up position with just one move, instead of two as with the usual shimari.

The temptation, even for certain professionals, is to use the hoshi stones of the sanrensei to make territory, but this is the wrong way to go.

This second chapter shows the real point of the sanrensei.

Game 1: Sanrensei and a large moyo

Even game played in 1985 between
Takemiya Masaki 9-dan, Black, and
Cho Chikun, Kisei, White.

There are two ways of playing when confronted with a large moyo. Some players make as many points as possible and then invade, while others invade immediately.

Typically, Mr Cho chooses the first option. So, as I really like to make a moyo, a game against him inevitably leads to an all-deciding central battle.

Here is an example.

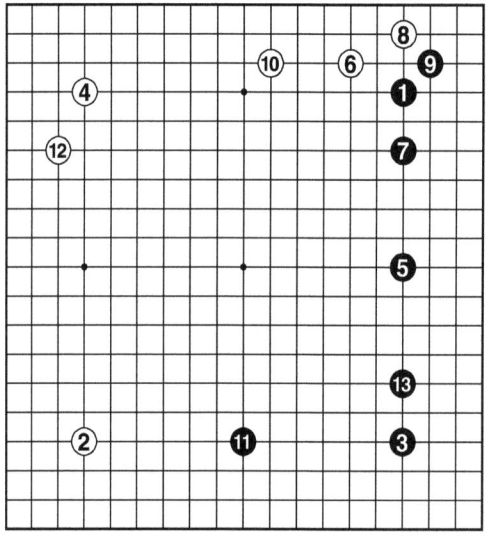

Figure 1 (1 – 13)

Figure 1
White 12 is typical of Mr Cho's style.

Diagram 1
Playing White 12 in 1 is also possible.

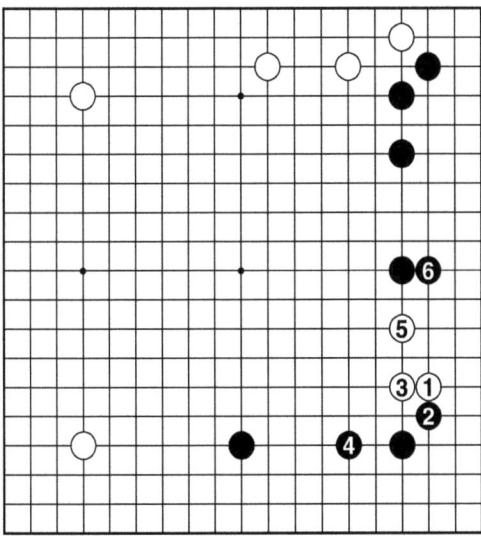

Dia. 1

Figure 2

After White 14, Black occupies the last large area with 15 and 17. This is a satisfactory fuseki for Black. Next, White invades Black's moyo with 18. Look closely at Black's answer: Black makes a kosumi with 19 and then, when White attaches at 20, plays the sequence 21 to 29. None of these moves are difficult. Some people think that go is mostly about finding nice tesuji. But go is not so complicated: just play natural moves in the right direction and you will never fall behind.

However, the game becomes more and more complicated when one doesn't play natural moves.

What is the natural direction for Black in this particular game? Surely it is to make a moyo with the sanrensei. You can play wherever you want to if you just follow this idea; it will work!

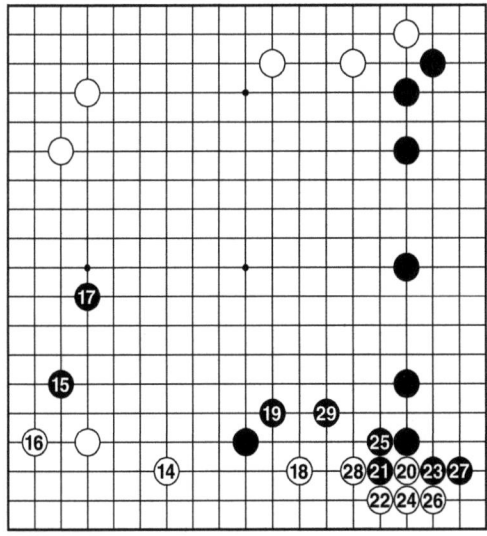

Figure 2 (14 – 29)

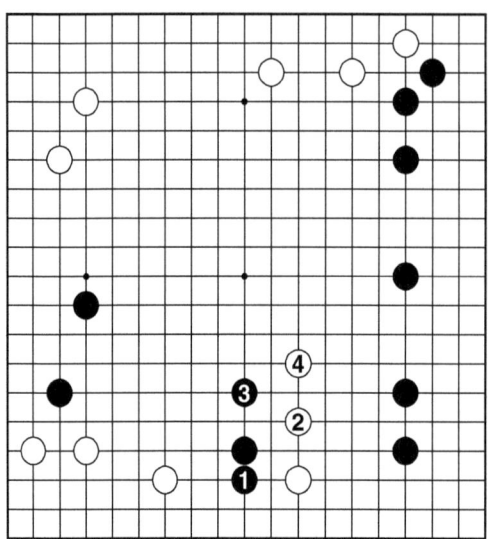

Dia. 2

Diagram 2

Answering White's invasion with a tetchu at 1 is very bad. White plays two tobis at 2 and 4, and Black loses all central influence.

Figure 3

White 30 is also typical of Mr Cho's style. Usually, players invade the moyo early on in the game. However, he prefers to let the moyo develop for quite a while before invading at the last minute.

One must play 31 somewhere in this region; I think that Black 31 is well placed.

With the sanrensei, it is important to make one's moyo as large as possible. A small moyo will not be invaded by your opponent. The right strategy is to make a big moyo and wait for the opponent to invade.

White played a kikashi at 32, and then finally took the plunge with 34! However, you now may ask yourself "I'd like to capture this White stone. But what shall I do if my attack fails and White escapes?"

Perhaps this position worries you?

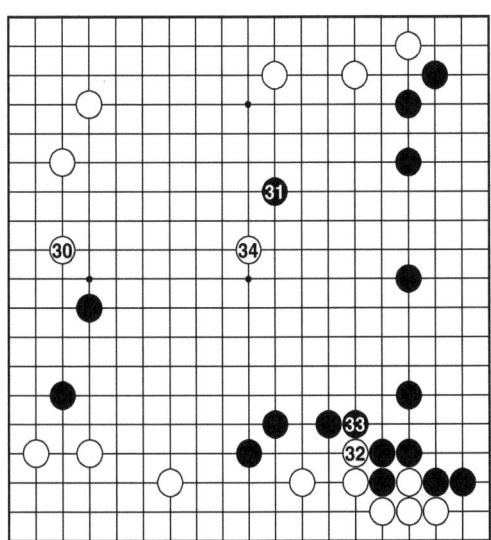

Figure 3 (30 – 34)

Do not try too hard to capture this stone, as if you do not succeed in capturing it you will just lose. What a shame…

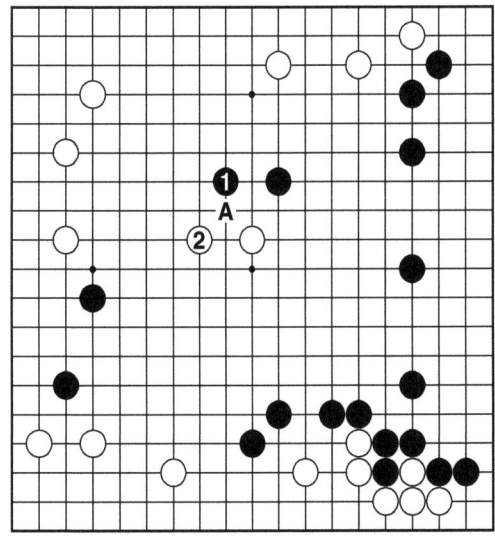

Dia. 3

Diagram 3

For example, let us suppose Black plays the tobi 1. Of course, White will also play a tobi at 2, and then Black has no follow-up.

Instead of attacking with 1, attacking with 2 doesn't work either: White would answer at A. This is no better.

These direct attacks do not give a good result.

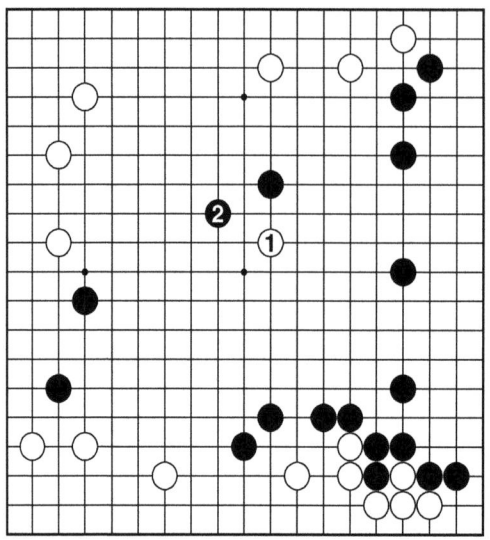

Dia. 4

Diagram 4

The choice would be clear if White had played 34 at 1 here. Black immediately attacks with 2.

This difference of one line is important. But you will not learn from deep reading; one knows this from 'feeling'.

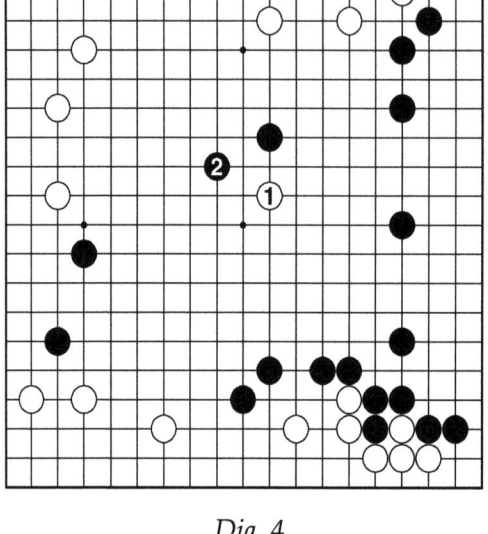

Dia. 5

Diagram 5

How about answering the White invasion ⊘ at 1? This is just another matter of 'feeling'. Just one glance tells me that this is bad for Black. It looks as if the big black moyo is crying.

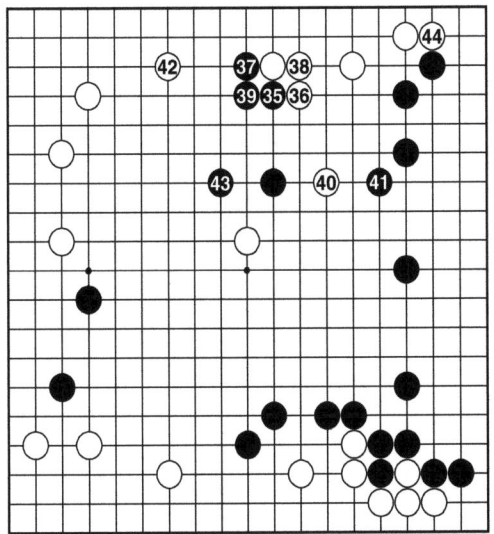

Figure 4 (35 – 44)

Figure 4

We have tried direct attack, and defence; neither works. So, what should one do?

A 'leaning attack' is useful in this sort of situation.

A good strategy when an attack on a stone does not work well is to 'lean' on other stones. Attaching with the tsuke at 35 follows this strategy.

After White's hane at 36, Black calmly reduces the white group's vital space with 37 and 39. On the one hand, Black cannot directly attack the central white stone, but on the other hand, neither can White connect this stone to another group with just one move.

Had White played 42 somewhere in the centre, his central stone would have been reinforced. But he preferred to take points along the side. With the tobi at 43, the central stone is weakened. This is one of the results of the 'leaning attack'. White even has to add 44…

I would like to show you an example where the result is worse for White.

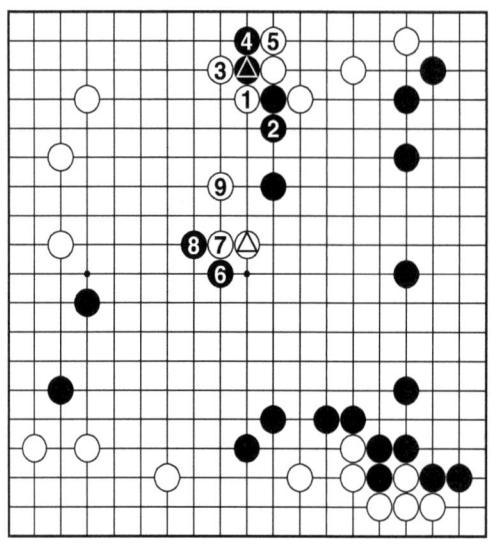

Dia. 6

Diagram 6

What should Black do if White plays violently with 1, 3 and 5 after Black's hane marked ▲?

Black attacks the central stone ⬭ from the other side with 6 and 8.

After 9...

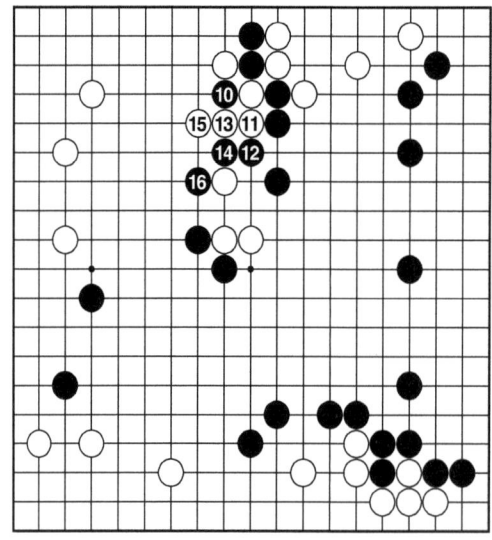

Dia. 7

Diagram 7

...Black cuts at 10. With the sequence up to 16, Black succeeds in cutting off White's group and closing in the three white stones in the centre.

This is just a simple example of how the stone ⬭ in Diagram 6 limits White's options.

This is a good example of how a 'leaning attack' works.

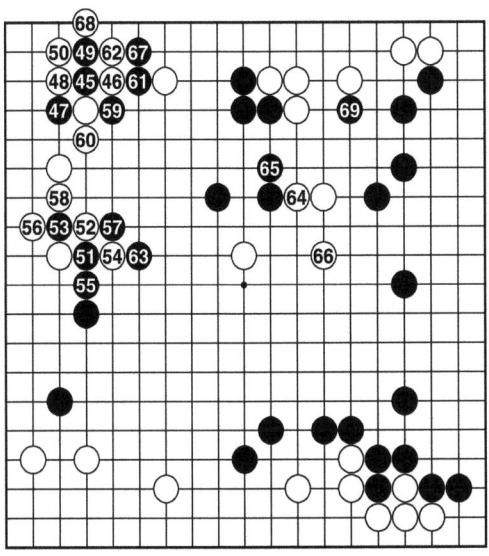

Figure 5 (*45 – 69*)

Figure 5

Black carries out more 'leaning attacks' with move 45 to 63. With 63, Black captures one stone; his strategy is working. White tries his best to resist with 64 and 66, but can no longer connect his group after Black 69.

In the continuation, White will try to live in the centre, but Black can kill him and thus win the game.

The way I killed the White group is less interesting than the way I prepared my attack.

Learn the 'leaning attack'; it will come in useful for your own games.

Result: White resigns.

Game 2: Think for yourself

Even game played in 1985 between
Takemiya Masaki 9-dan, Black, and
Cho Chikun, Kisei, White.

This is another unforgettable game with Mr Cho.

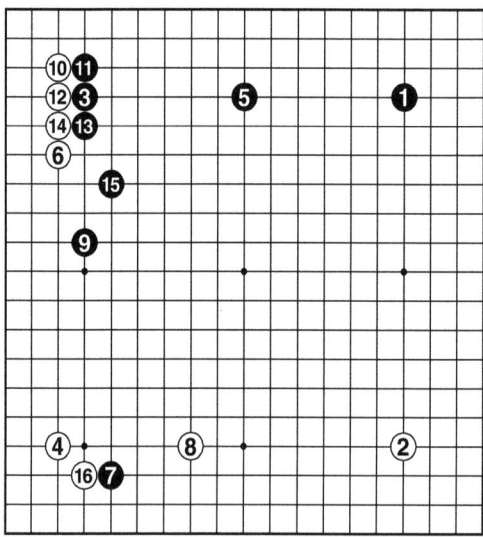

Figure 1 (1 – 16)

Figure 1

As usual I choose the sanrensei for its central influence. White takes territory with 12 and 14. Black can also play 15 as in Diagram 1.

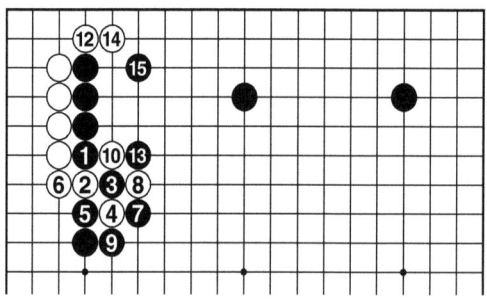

Dia. 1 (11 at 4)

Diagram 1

Here White makes a few points with 12 and 14, but Black is happy to get outside influence with 13 and 15.

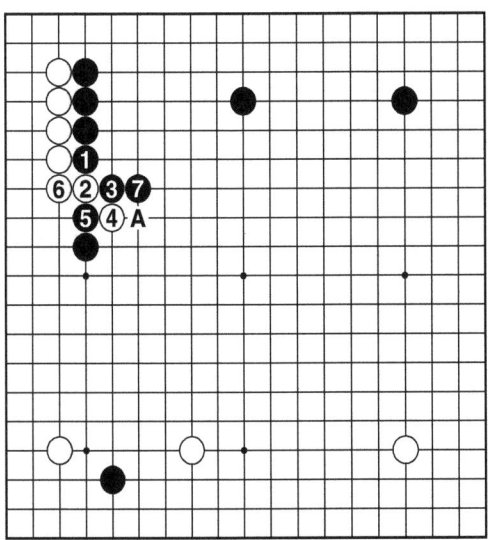

Dia. 2

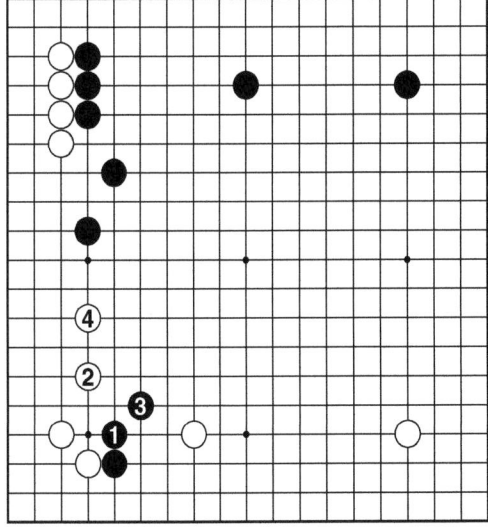

Dia. 3

Diagram 2

This variation is also a joseki. Black makes more points than in Diagram 1, but later on White can activate his stone at 4 by playing at A. This weakness is unpleasant for Black.

I prefer the sequence in Dia 1. Perhaps this is a matter of taste.

Back to the game: how should one answer White 16?

Diagram 3

The nobi 1 is a 'common sense' move, but as you know, I dislike 'common sense'.

You will find plenty of books recommending this move. Nonetheless, it is a bad move in this situation. White is happy to play 2 and 4. One glance suffices to see that the Black group is heavy.

At this point, the most important thing on the goban is Black's moyo, based on the sanrensei.

If Black plays as in this Diagram, White can use an attack on the weak and heavy black group on the lower side to destroy Black's moyo. This is dangerous.

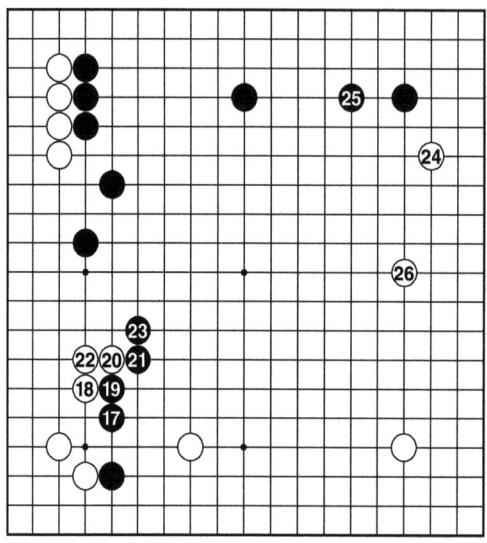

Figure 2 (17 – 26)

Figure 2

I decided to play 17. White plays 18 and Black answers at 19, and then makes a good shape with 21 and 23. This is satisfactory for Black. Next, White occupies the right-hand side; this is very big.

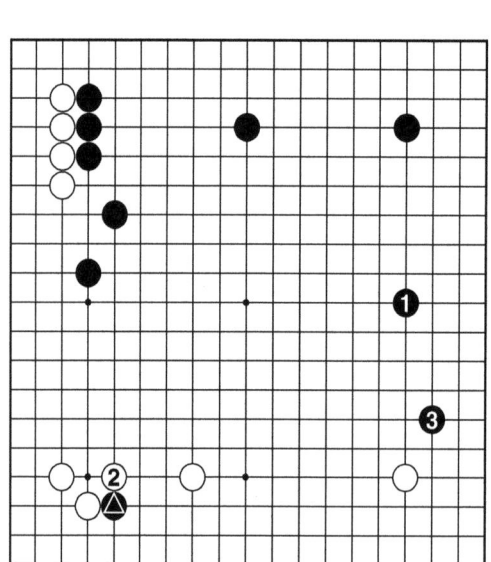

Dia. 4

Diagram 4

Another idea for 17 in the game is to occupy the right side of the goban with 1 and 3. The loss of the ⬣ stone is not too big. This is a very dynamic moyo strategy based upon the sanrensei.

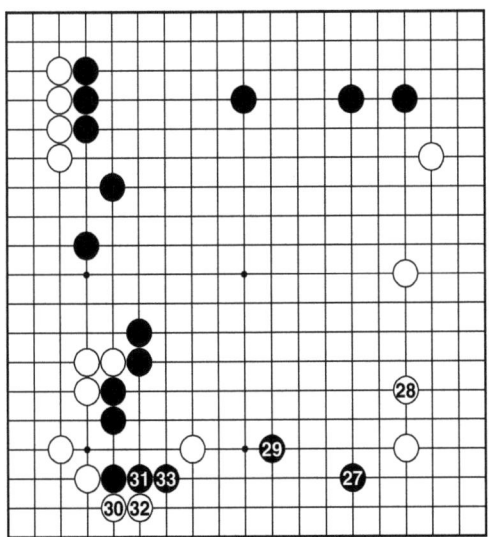

Figure 3 (27 – 33)

Figure 3

Next, as White has occupied the right side, Black occupies the lower side with 27 and 29. However, the sequence 27 to 29 is not good, as White plays two kikashi: 30 and 32. Now Black's stones at the bottom have become over-concentrated.

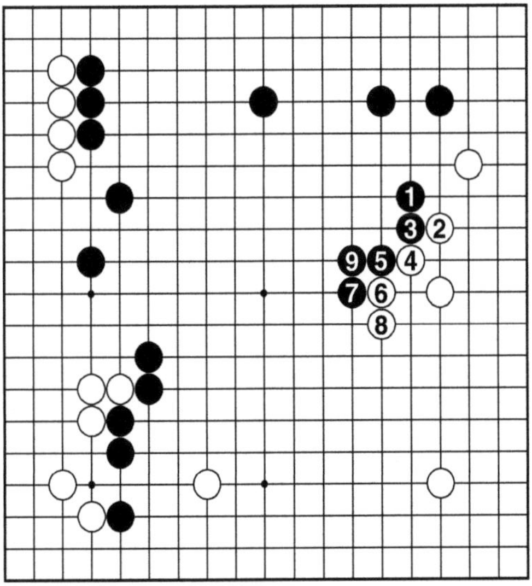

Dia. 5

Diagram 5

Developing the moyo with 1 in this Diagram is better than 27 in the figure. One can imagine the continuation up to 9.

In a moyo game, it is often better to occupy the centre instead of a side. Once again this goes against 'common sense', but in cosmic go there is no such thing as 'common sense'.

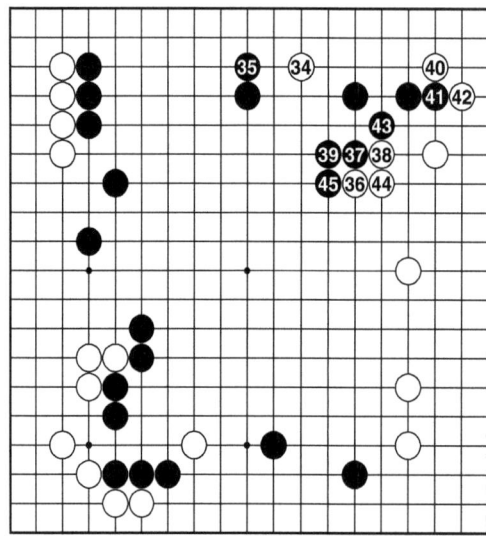

Figure 4 (34 – 45)

Figure 4

Go is a game of combat between two personalities. A game between Mr Cho and myself often leads to violent invasions and fighting. We both have faith in our own ways of playing, so this is only natural.

Often the game ends with a struggle where one player tries to kill an enemy group and the other tries to save it.

Perhaps our games are so exciting because we both play the moves that please us. I do hope that you too play moves that please you.

White's invasion with 34 starts the middle-game fighting. Mr Cho found it dangerous to save his stone at 34 directly, and so played 36.

Black then builds a big territory from the tsuke at 37 through to 45. Black is undoubtedly in the lead.

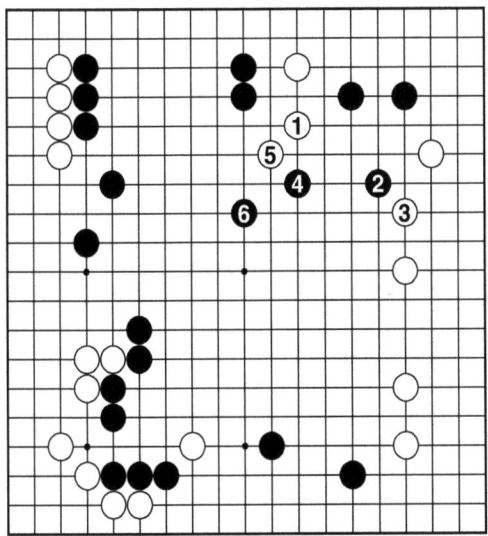

Dia. 6

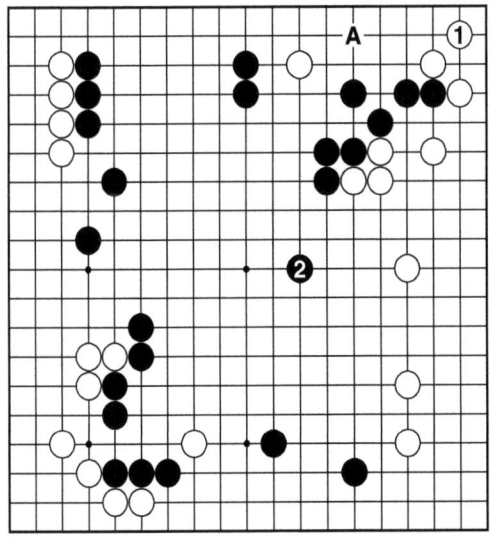

Dia. 7

Diagram 6

Perhaps some people may wonder why White didn't move out towards the centre with 1. To do so would be to fall into Black's trap. When Black attacks with the sequence from 2 to 6, White cannot survive. White could play 3 at 4, but then Black would be happy to destroy White's forces on the right side. Clearly this is bad for White.

Back to the game: when White claims the corner with 40 and 42, Black plays tenuki and occupies the centre with 43 and 45. The idea is simple and good.

Diagram 7

Players keen on joseki may wonder why White did not then play 1. The reason is that Black can play tenuki and push further into the centre with 2.

It is true that 1 does give White a very big yose move at A, but one needs to look at the situation globally: does this corner seem so important, compared with the centre?

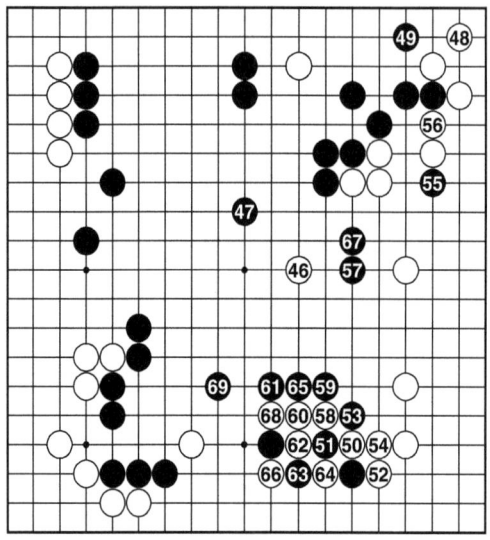

Figure 5   (46 – 69)

Figure 5

Black 47: this move is too slow and too easygoing. I do in general try to play moves that please me, without worrying about the result of the game. But when the desire to win becomes too strong I can play bad moves like 47. Instead of 47, playing a tobi at 53 would be much more dynamic, and goes well with my style.

I cannot play fine games if I am too concerned with winning.

In the game, White quickly plays 50 and 52; Black is now in a difficult position. Even so, when White cuts at 58, I had the tesuji 59 and 61 that allowed me to make a large territory. The game is now very close.

There is no such thing as 'common sense' in go. Rather than relying on joseki, one must think for oneself. Move 17 in this game, the black tobi, is a good example of this.

Result: White resigns.

Game 3: Large-scale sanrensei

Even game played in 1990 between
Takemiya Masaki 9-dan, Black, and
Cho Chikun, Judan, White.

Here is another game against Mr Cho. This game shows my dream for the centre.

Figure 1

In this figure, move 9 is not a misprint! Black 9 aims at the capping move (boshi) 11. I played 9 quickly, without thinking, instinctively. In the go magazine 'Kido', this move was presented as an unprecedent novelty. Yet it was a very natural move for me.

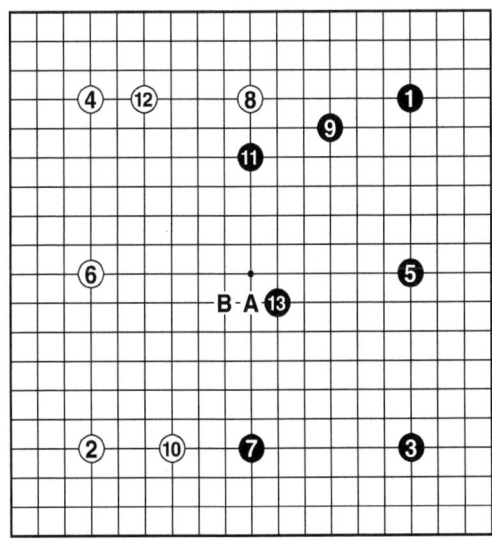

I should have played 13 at A or B, this would have been much more dynamic.

Figure 1 (1 – 13)

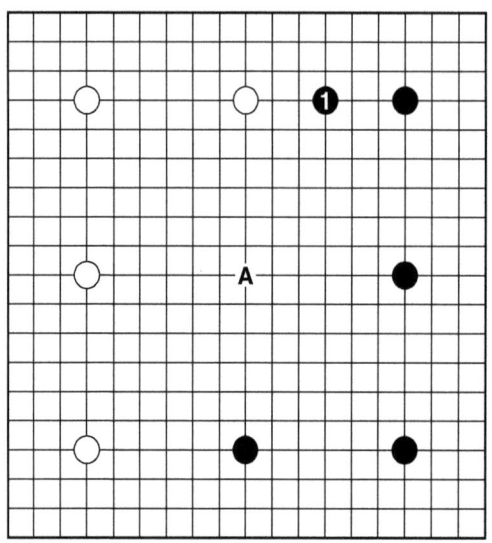

Dia. 1

Diagram 1

Normally, Black plays 1 or at A. This would give a different game.

The problem with 1 is that there is no good follow-up for Black.

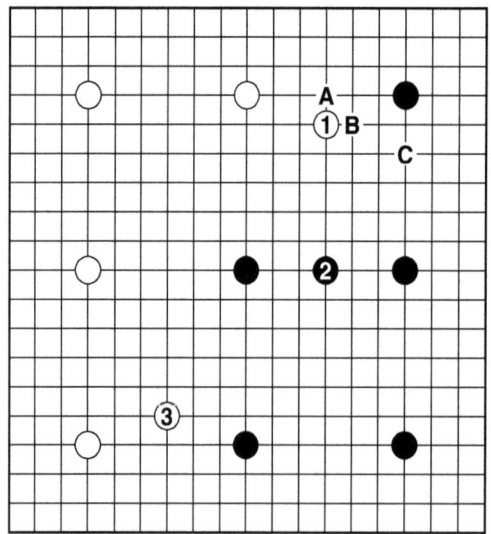

Dia. 2

Diagram 2

Actually, in a different game against the great Shuko Fujisawa, I had already played White 1 – a move that had shocked the spectators. Given Mr Shuko's style, if I had played the usual move at A, he would surely have played B. This is why I played 1.

My worthy opponent preferred to occupy the centre with 2, instead of the usual response at C. I was happy to have an original game, and continued with another unusual move: 3.

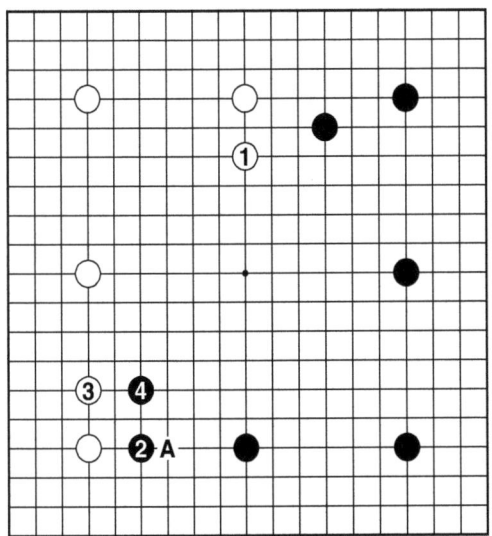

Dia. 3

Diagram 3

Let's go back to the game with Mr Cho. White could have played a tobi at 1 to avoid being capped. Instead, he chose to build territory with A while allowing me to develop a large central moyo. This is very much Mr Cho's style.

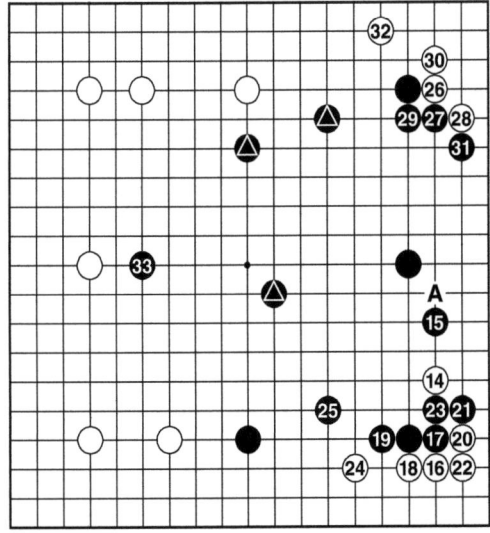

Figure 2 (14 – 33)

Figure 2

When White approaches at 14, the pincer at 15 is another move that disregards 'common sense'. According to reference books, 15 is too slow, as White can simply take the san-san, with 16.

However, I found that 15 was the right way to activate the three stones marked ⬤.

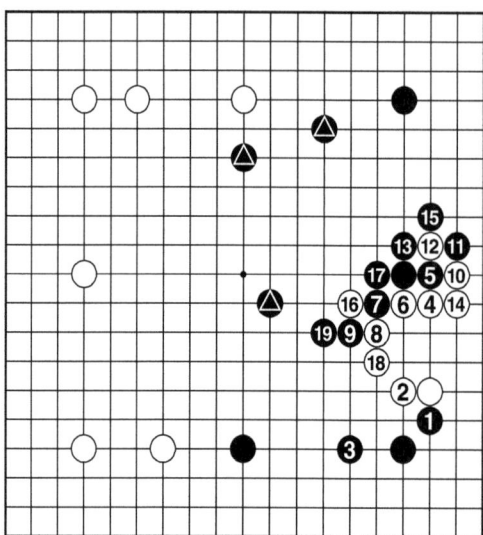

Dia. 4

Diagram 4

The book-move, kosumi-tsuke at 1 is not good. White makes sabaki with 4 to 12. After 19, one can see that the ⬤ stones are not working at all. Black 1 is in fact much too slow!

Compare this result with the game, where after 25 the ⬤ stones really shine, thanks to the pincer at 15.

Next, White invades the top right corner with 26 to 32, but I felt fine after capping once more with 33. Notice that with the same sequence, 15 would be even better placed at A.

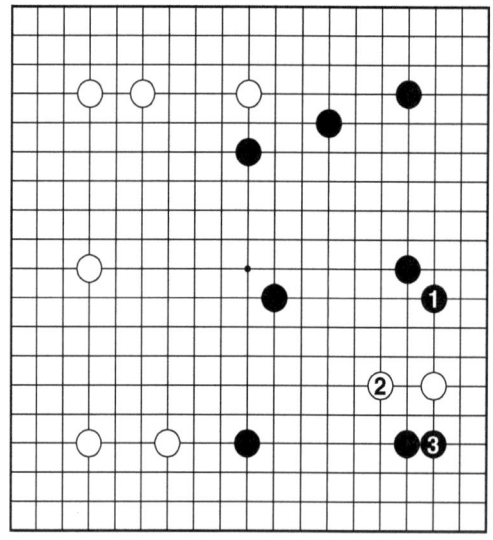

Dia. 5

Diagram 5

Here is a position from another game I played with Mr Cho recently. White has just played an approach move (kakari); my answer was the kosumi at 1. Since Mr Cho didn't want to take the corner by playing at the san-san, he played the tobi 2. Black 3 then took away the white group's eye space, and this began a difficult fight.

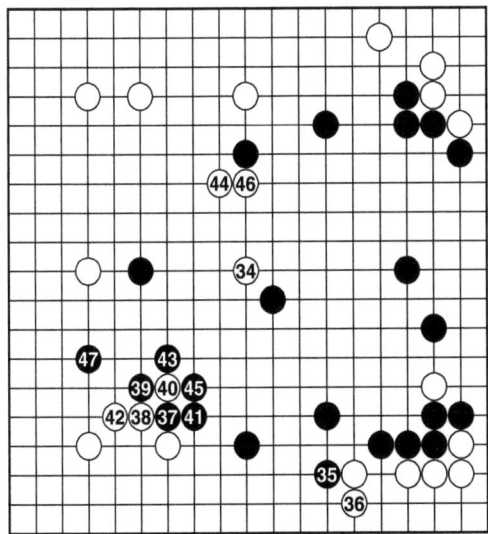

Figure 3 (34 – 47)

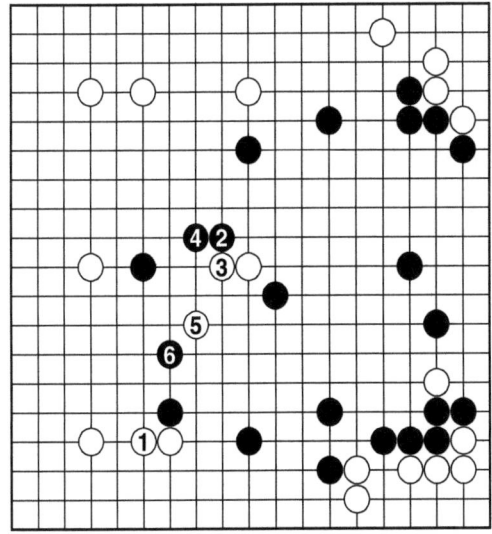

Dia. 6

Once again, I say to you: do not believe in common sense. Do not blindly follow joseki, they do not always work. Rather, believe in your own intuition.

Figure 3

Finally White invades with 34. How should Black respond? Here the 'leaning attack' is the correct strategy. The Black tsuke 37 is an example of a technique often used in leaning attacks. White consolidates his central group with 44 and 46, but the ponnuki Black makes with 45 is a very solid shape. Black is satisfied with the result after 47.

Diagram 6

Simply playing at 1 in response to the tsuke at 37 would be dangerous for White. Black could close White in with 2 to 6.

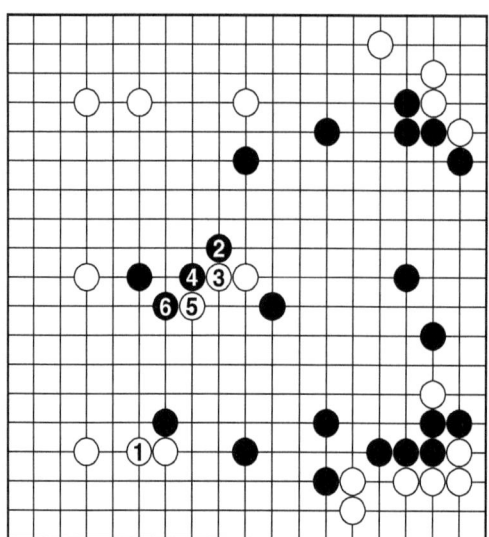

Diagram 7

Another option would be the double hane in Diagram 7. This is even more severe.

Dia. 7

How do you find this game? I always want to fascinate people with my games. Mr Nagashima in baseball, and Mr Osaki Shoji in golf, are both popular because they try to play in a very dynamic way that goes beyond common sense. It fascinates people.

These sportsmen inspire me. While respecting go's inherent beauty, I try to play moves that will move people. With this in mind, a game's result is clearly secondary.

Result: White resigns.

Game 4: The flexible sanrensei

Even game played in 1990 between
Takemiya Masaki 9-dan,Black, and
Cho Hunhyun 9-dan, White.

Here is the sort of remark one often hears "I try to make a large moyo, but my opponent stops me."

However, I repeat that the cosmic style is a natural style. If my opponent tries to make territory, my stones naturally tend towards the centre. But my opponent may also be interested in the centre, and then I must be flexible. Flexible judgment is part of the cosmic style.

The following game is a good example of this kind of problem.

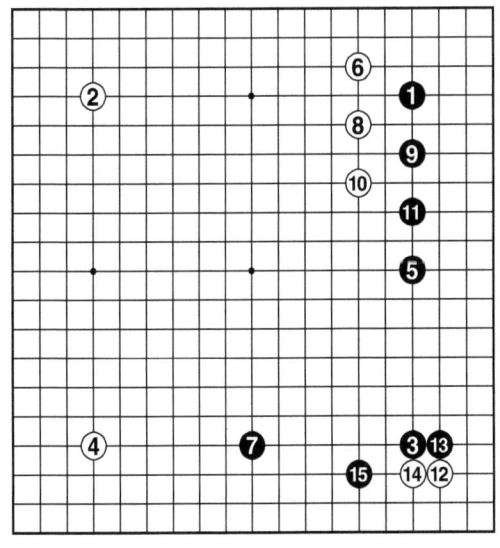

Figure 1 (1 – 15)

Figure 1

When White approaches with 6 (kakari), I tenuki and take a fourth hoshi with 7 (yon-ren-sei).

Mr Cho then chose to counter the sanrensei by playing two tobi, at 8 and 10, preventing Black from making a large moyo.

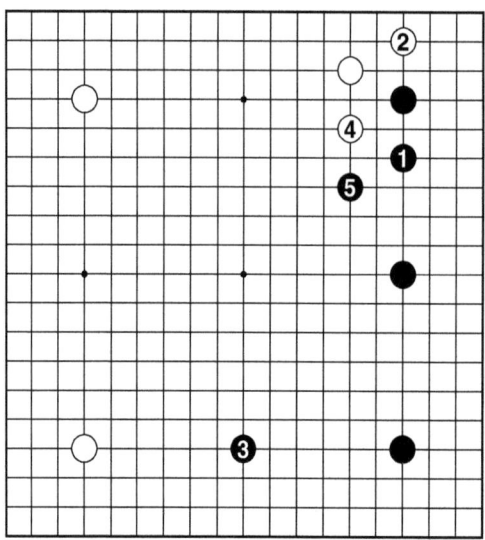

Dia. 1

Diagram 1

To avoid this, Black could have answered at 1 (instead of 7 in the game). If White plays 2, then Black takes the fourth hoshi with 3. Moves 8 and 10 of the game are better placed for White than moves 2 and 4 in the Diagram.

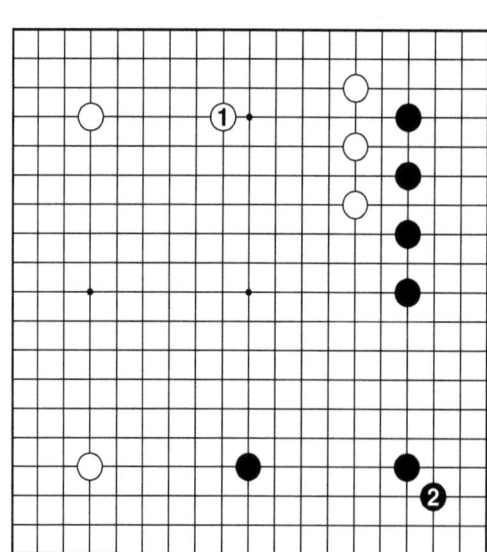

Dia. 2

In the game, White 12 is quite true to Mr Cho's style: first limit the enemy moyo and then take territory.

Diagram 2

However, making an extension with 1 is calmer and more natural.

For me, a difficult question is then whether to play at 2, or elsewhere.

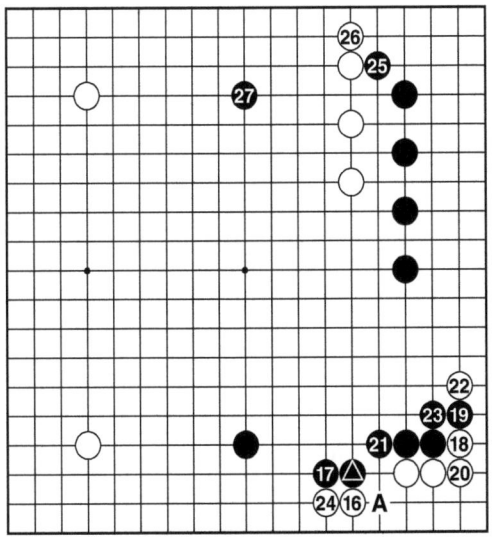

Figure 2 (16 – 27)

Figure 2

Move 15 (△) is unusual, but there is no need to learn this move by heart. I chose to play 15 so as to gain sente. In fact, each move played up to 23 aimed at gaining sente.

For instance...

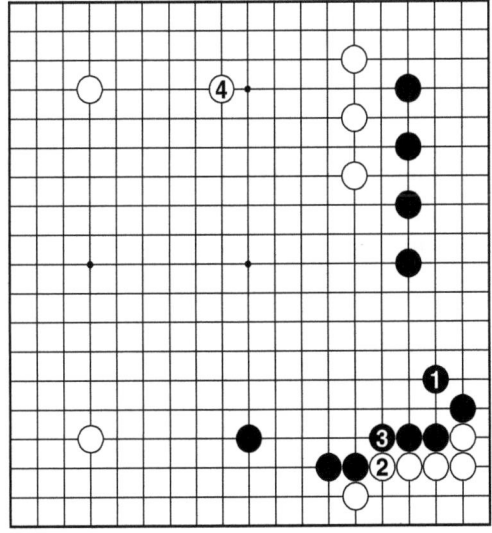

Dia. 3

Diagram 3

...if I had connected with 1, White would have played kikashi at 2 and then made a good extension with 4.

In the game, White 24 is not forced. However, without this move, Black can capture the stone at 16 by playing A. This puts White in a difficult position: his invasion at the san-san is no longer justified.

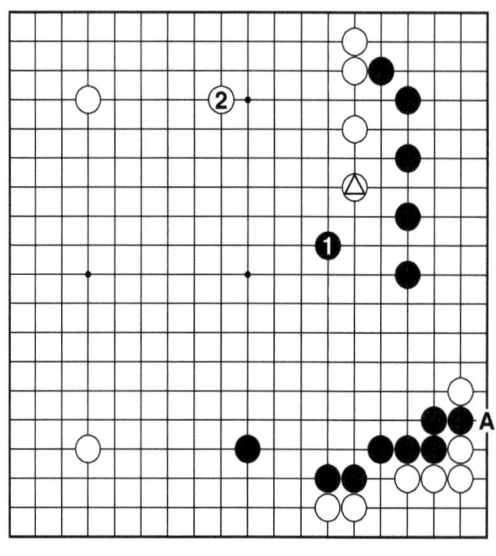

Dia. 4

Diagram 4

Given that Black has chosen the sanrensei, an opening that favours central influence, one might find 1 natural.

In fact, however, this is a really bad idea!

The right side has already been limited by the White tobi marked △. It is not at all natural then to want to develop this area.

White would be happy to play 2. Such a small moyo will never frighten your opponent; particularly as White can very easily invade with A.

So where is the natural move in this situation?

One has to look at the top side, where White has not yet made an extension from his wall. Black 27 is the vital point!

The disappointment of not being able to carry out the sanrensei large-moyo strategy is largely compensated by getting an attack on the white stones. One needs good intuition, but above all, one must be flexible.

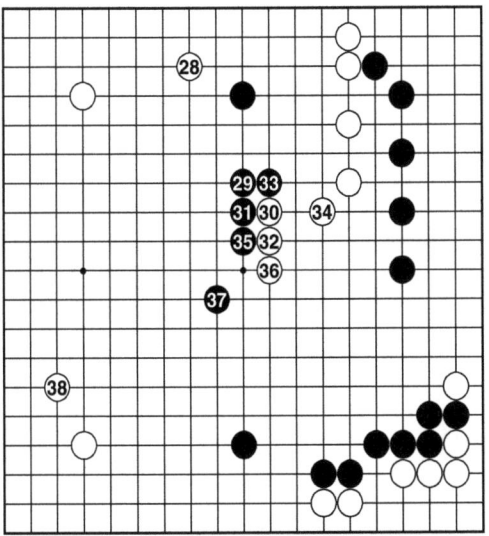

Figure 3 (28 – 38)

Figure 3

White played 28 and I played a tobi at 29; the structure of this game was becoming clear. With an attack against the top right white group, I should be in the lead. Territory will come naturally if I simply attack.

I was pleased to see White 30. I pushed once with 31 and then played the magari at 33; I felt on top of the world.

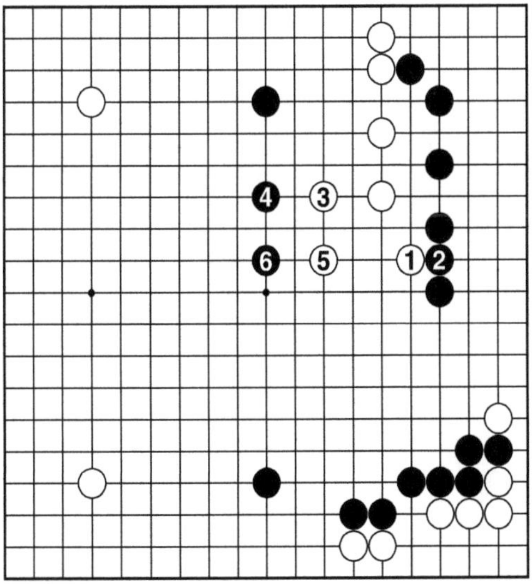

Diagram 5

Instead of playing 30, White could have played nozoki at 1, and then made a good shape with 3 and 5.

This very interesting idea was suggested by Mr Shuko Fujisawa, for whom I have the greatest respect.

Dia. 5

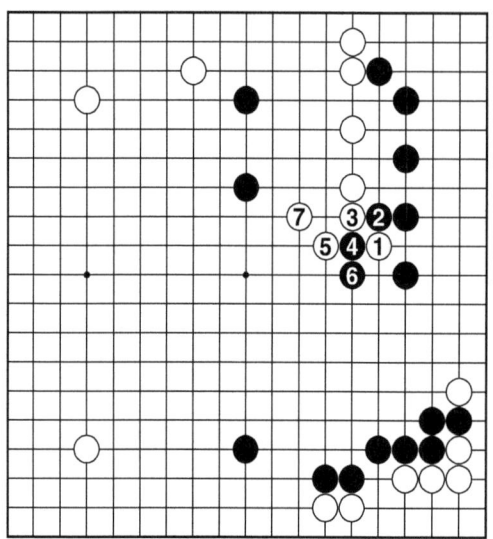

Dia. 6

Diagram 6

After the White nozoki 1, if Black cuts with 2 and 4, White makes good shape with 5 and 7.

I would automatically answer this nozoki by connecting.

In the game, I move out into the centre with 35 and 37 while continuing to attack; I feel fine in this position.

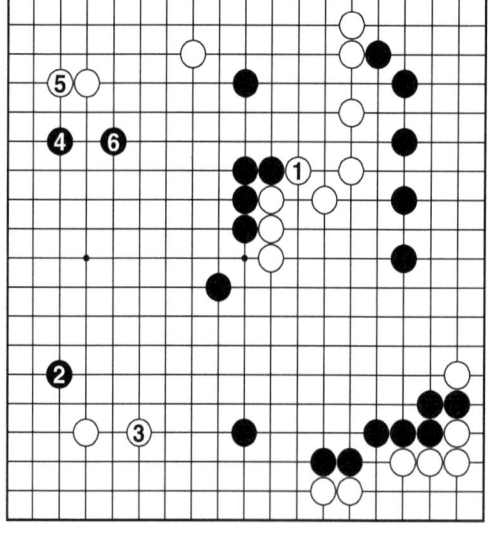

Dia. 7

Diagram 7

If White plays 38 at 1 in this Diagram, Black constructs a large-scale moyo with 2, 4 and 6.

One could not foresee this moyo at the beginning of the game; it was built thanks to the attack on White's group.

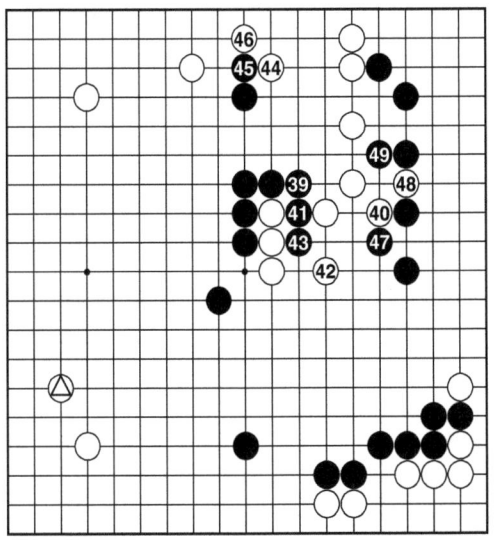

Figure 4 (39 – 49)

Figure 4

White takes territory with 38 (⊘) but don't worry: Black will be compensated by attacking, with 39 onwards.

Despite White 40, Black moves forward with 41 and 43. I think that, at this point in the game, certain professionals will already start counting territories. With the cosmic style, I trust more in feeling than in calculation.

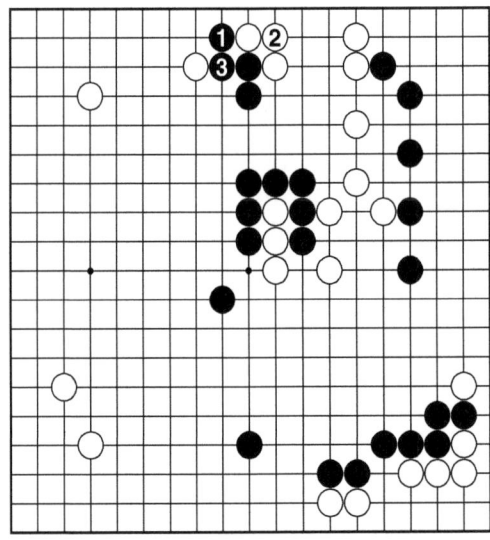

Dia. 8

Diagram 8

In order to handle 44 and 46, I had initially thought of the simple moves 1 and 3 in this Diagram. These are in fact not bad moves. However, it seems I was filled with kiai (fighting spirit), as I chose the severest moves in this situation: 47 and 49.

I was told that many people were astonished by 49.

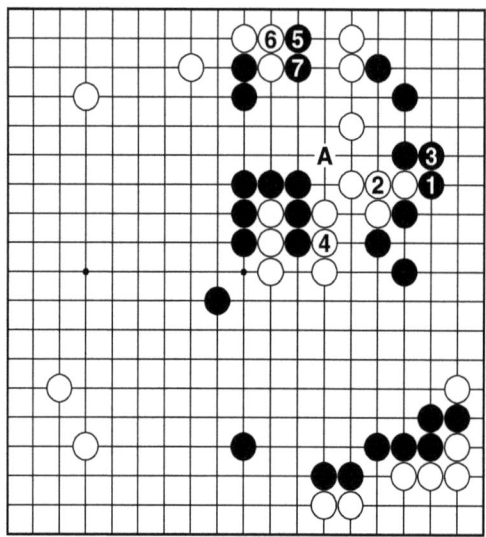

Dia. 9

Diagram 9

It is true that simply play-ing 1 and 3 is correct. With the kikashi at A, 5 also works well.

However, I changed my mind during the game.

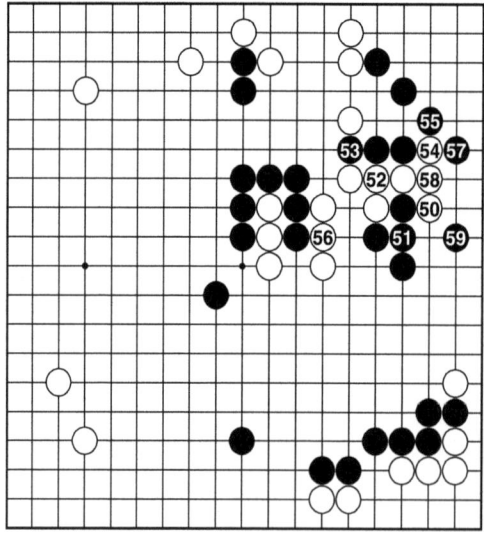

Figure 5 (50 – 59)

Figure 5

With the sequence up to 53, Black succeeds in cutting the White group in two. I believe my choice is more dynamic than the preceding Diagrams.

Let me assure you that I am not trying to kill White.

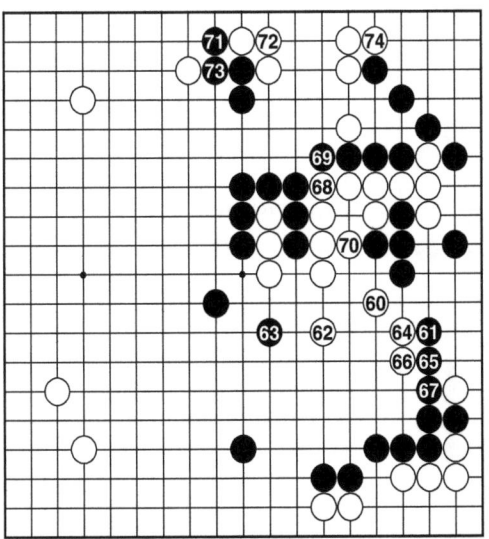

Figure 6 (60 – 73)

Figure 6

How surprising – White has managed to live!

Even when they see the rest of the game, many players find the result good for White.

Even Mr Cho, as he played them, found these moves good for White.

However, I find the sequence painful for White.

I cannot stand having to live, as White does, with two small eyes, when there are so many other attractive points on the goban.

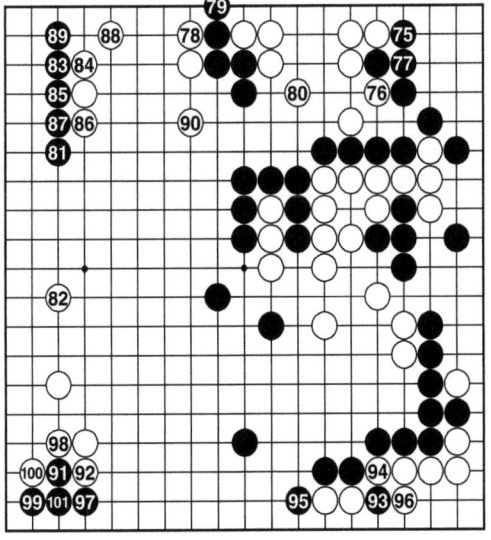

Figure 7 (74 – 101)

Figure 7

So, I was very happy for Black when White made a small life with 80. There is no need to count in this position: Black is in the lead because he has better shape.

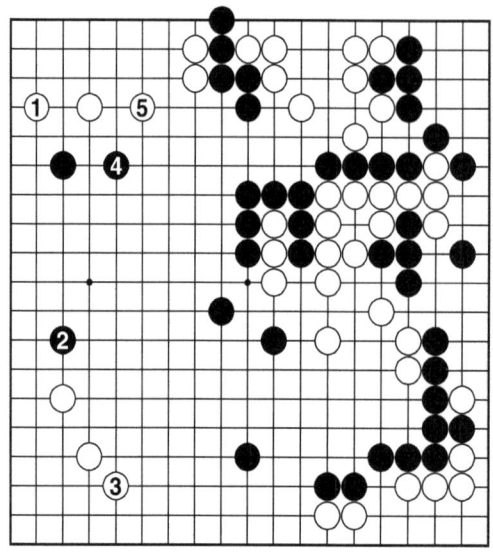

Dia. 10

Diagram 10

White 1 in this Diagram is better than 82 in the game. One can predict the continuation up to 5. This Diagram is less good for Black than the game.

In the game, Black invades the corner in sente with 83 and gets to play at the san-san with 91 as well. Black has a large lead on White.

Cautious players who only believe in figures can count; they will see the result for themselves.

If one of your opponents' priorities is the centre, I hope you can say to yourself: "Oh well, never mind". Try to stay relaxed and adapt your strategy flexibly. You shouldn't lose all your games if you choose the cosmic style and your opponent doesn't let you make a central moyo. I do not believe the cosmic style is as poor as that...

Result: Black wins by 3½ points.

Game 5: Play small or play big

Even game played in 1993 between
Takemiya Masaki, Judan, Black, and
Kobayashi Koichi, Kisei, White.

Although, like Mr Cho Chikun, Mr Kobayashi plays in a territorial manner, his style is different. While Mr Cho tends to let a moyo become very developed before he invades it, Mr Kobayashi prefers to invade early on. He plays very precise moves.

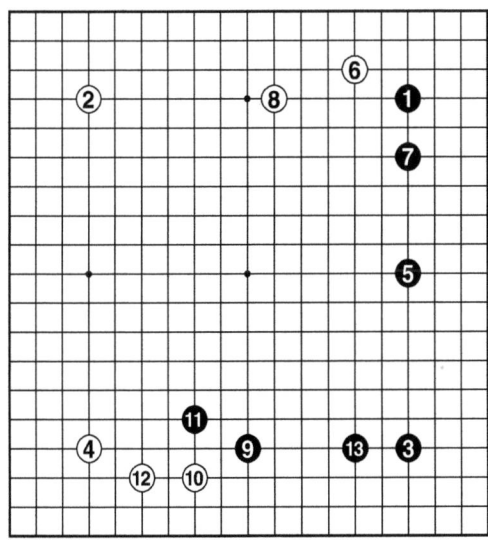

Figure 1

White 8 is the way Mr Kobayashi plays against a sanrensei.

Figure 1 (1 – 13)

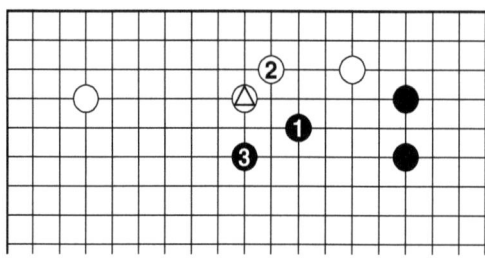

Dia. 1

Diagram 1

White usually plays the hoshi ⬯. But later on, Black can enlarge his moyo with 1 and 3. This is why White played 8 one space to the right of the hoshi. However, 8 also has its disadvantages.

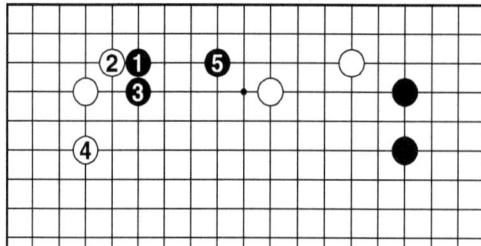

Dia. 2

Diagram 2

This is an easy way to invade the white area. Of course, one cannot clearly say if this is a good choice.

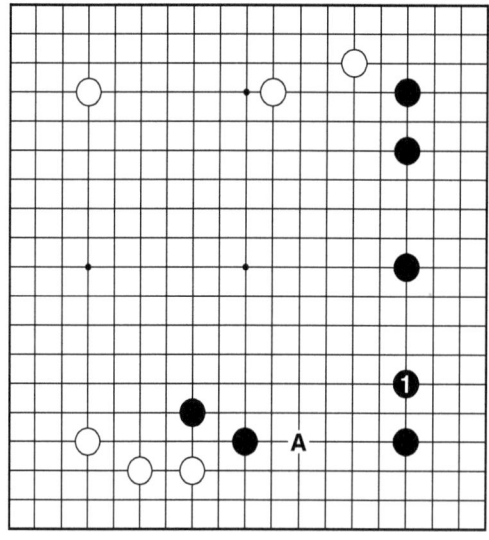

Dia. 3

Diagram 3

I put a lot of thought into Black 13.

One usually makes a shimari on the other side with 1. Next, White can start a fight by invading at A. This is quite a common fuseki.

However, I changed direction with 13. I cannot give you my reasons for this choice. I just wanted to play this way.

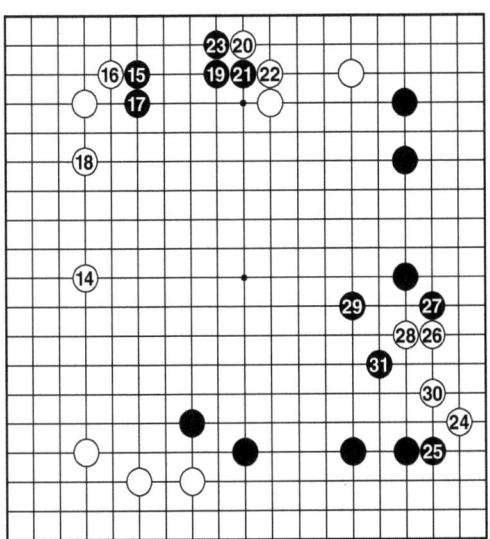

Figure 2 (14 – 31)

Figure 2 – Diagram 4

As I explained in the last page, Black 15 exploits the weakness in White 8.

The early invasion at 24 is in Mr Kobayashi's style. In this position, I would play differently, as in Diagram 4.

Black 25 is normal, but 27 and 29 are not my style.

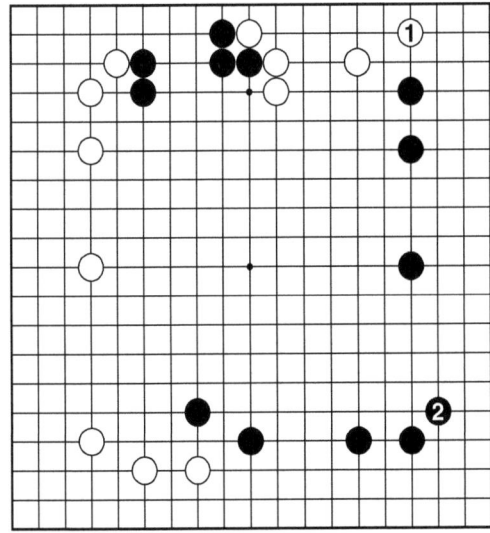

Dia. 4

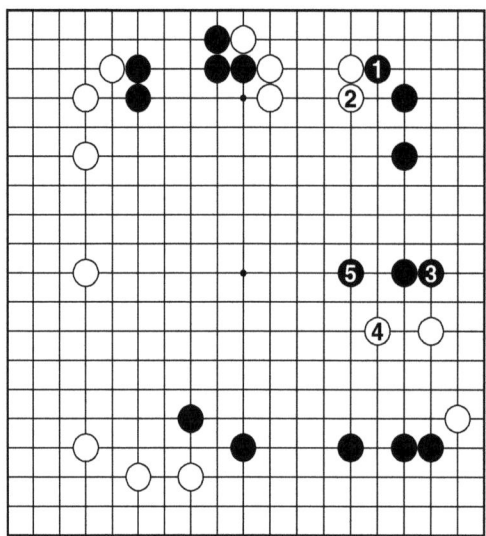

Diagram 5

Playing calmly with 1 to 5 is more my style.

Perhaps I played the very severe moves 27 and 29 as I felt too much like fighting. Actually, I still need to study these moves; they are not true to my style of play.

White 30 and Black 31 are both very important.

Dia. 5

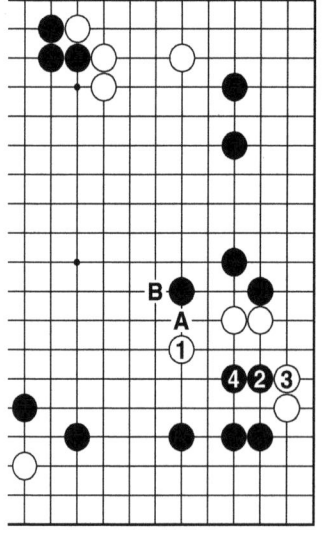

Diagram 6

If White plays 1, then 2, 3 and 4 follow. The white stone at 1 is then badly placed. Playing the tsuke at A instead of 1 is not good: Black simply plays the nobi at B.

This is why White played 30; Black answered with a keima at 31.

With this way of looking at things, we see that deep reading of sequences is not really necessary in go. You just need good knowledge of shape to see that Diagram 6 is bad for White; and to learn about shape, you must train your intuition.

Dia. 6

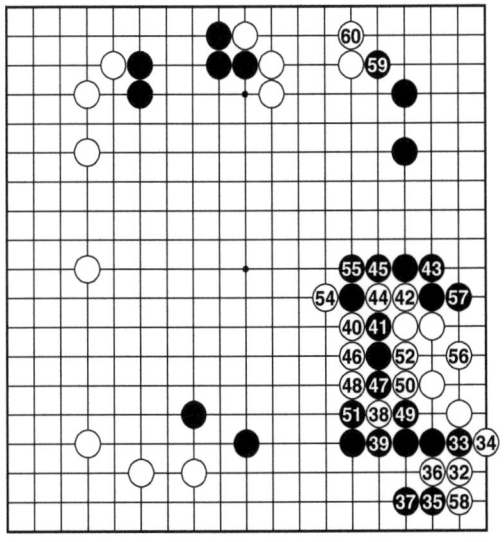

Figure 3   (32 – 60)

53 at 38

Figure 3

I had not foreseen White 32. The idea behind this move must be: "As my group has to live at any rate, it's better to live while reducing my opponent's territory as much as possible."

With 32, White harms his own eye space (see moves 33 and 35). In any case, I find this move inconceivable.

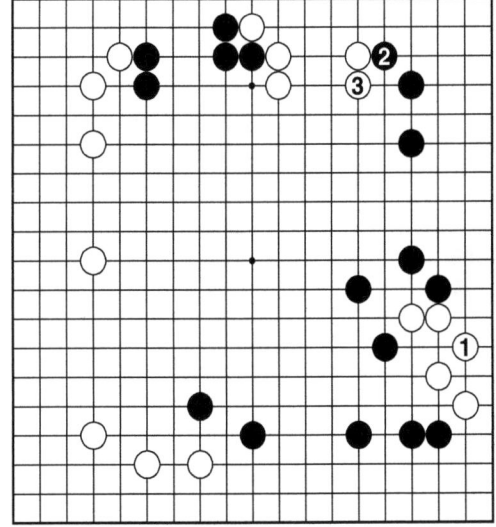

Dia. 7

Diagram 7

In White's place, I would calmly live with 1. Next would follow a kikashi at 2; only then would I ask myself how to play.

In the game, White manages to live with the sequence up to 58, but Black gains a great deal of central influence.

How do you evaluate this sequence?

I say Black gains a large lead on White.

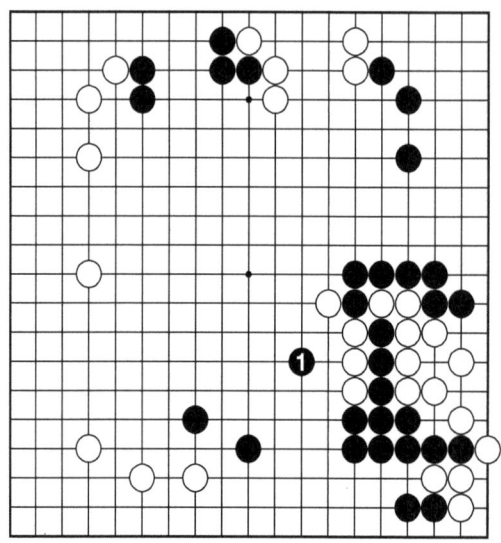

Dia. 8

Diagram 8

After the exchange of 59 for 60, the first thing that comes to mind is to capture White's stones in the centre with 1. But this does not give Black very much profit and does not make the most of Black's influence. This is the 'small' way of playing.

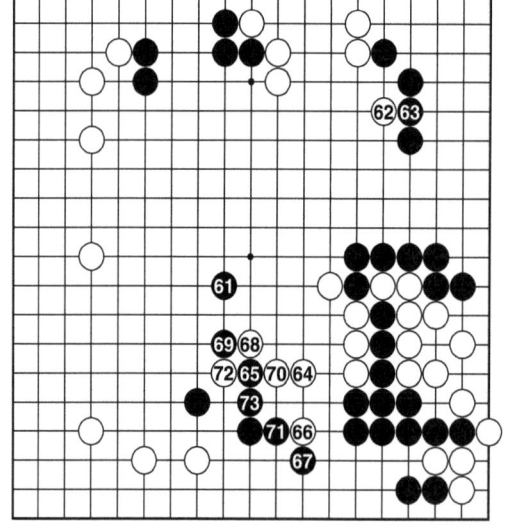

Figure 4 (61 – 73)

Figure 4

Here is Black 61! Do you feel the size of this move? This move seems to say: "Do live, as otherwise I shall take everything."

This grandeur is all-important. In moyo games, trying to kill enemy groups at all costs is the wrong strategy. The opponent can simply sacrifice them. Compare 61 with 1 in the previous Diagram.

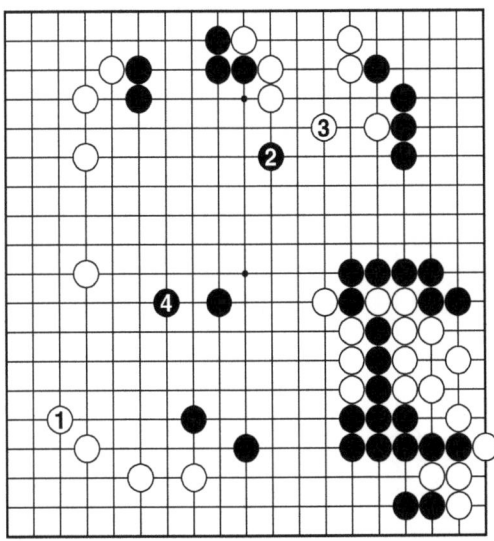

Dia. 9

Diagram 9

If White does not save his stones, Black continues to develop his central influence with 2 and 4.

White is therefore forced to save them and Black's strategy is then to consolidate his lead by attacking.

It is important here to abandon the idea of killing. If you can relax and say to yourself: "It's enough to let my opponent live while gaining something elsewhere," you will already have changed your point of view on go.

Nonetheless, even though I speak like a great master, I also play 65, which leaves bad aji.

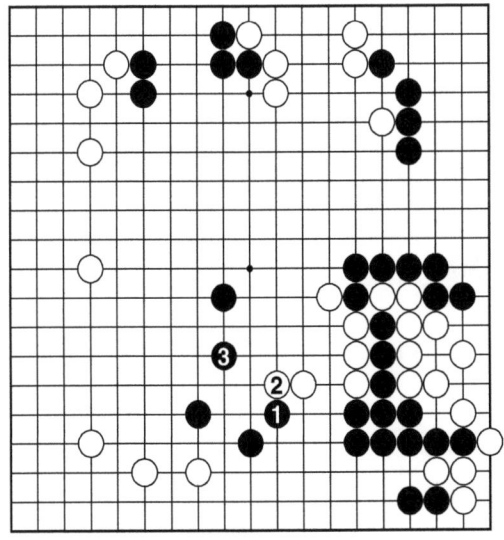

Dia. 10

Diagram 10

Instead of 65, the kosumi at 1 followed by 3 is better.

Even so, despite Black 65, White is still in trouble.

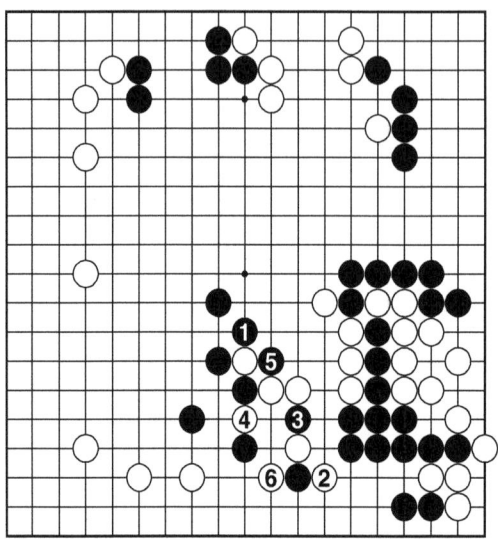

Dia. 11

Diagram 11

White 68 and 70 are played to stop Black from playing 1.

If Black plays 1, White destroys his territory on the lower side with 2, 4 and 6.

In the game, Black contains White with 71. He uses the attack to gain strength on all sides.

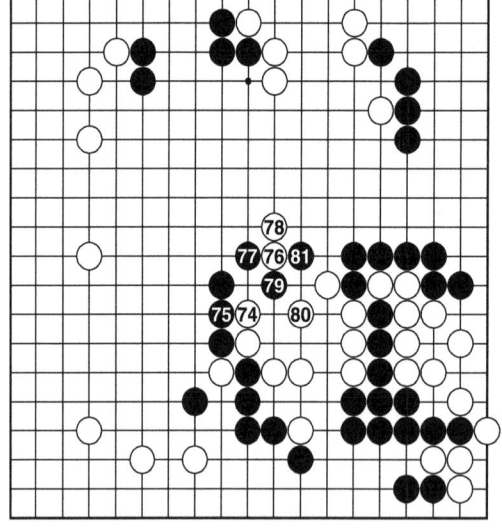

Figure 5 (74 – 81)

Figure 5

The nobi 74 is too cautious.

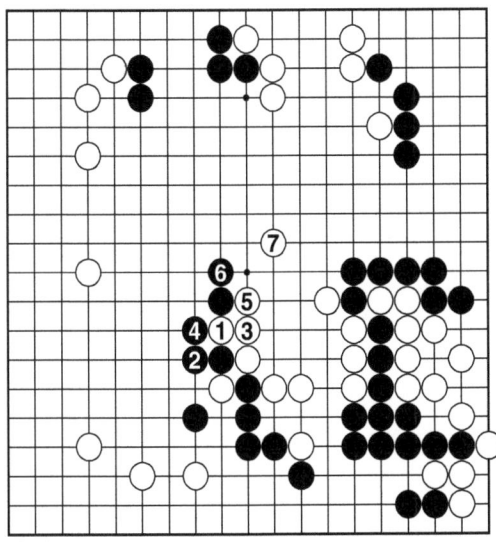

Dia. 12

Diagram 12

One should first give atari at 1 and then connect with 3. After 7, White is much better off than in the game.

Why didn't Mr Kobayashi play as in this Diagram?

In his commentary afterwards, he said he was afraid Black would play 2 and 4 as in Diagram 13. Such a problem worries him, as he too often lets his opponent make a ponnuki! In fact Black cannot let his opponent make a ponnuki and is absolutely forced to play 2 as in this Diagram.

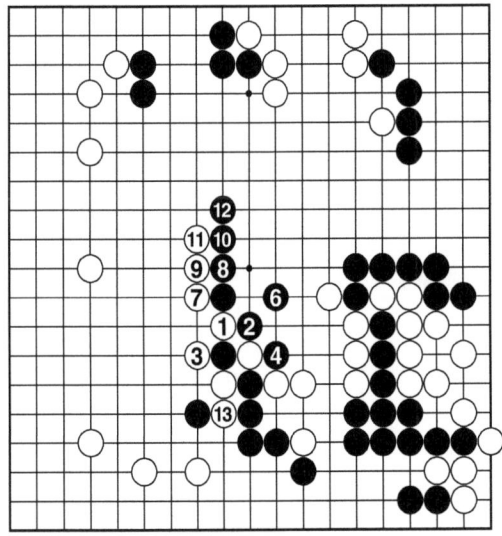

Dia. 13
5 connects below 1

Diagram 13

If White gets the ponnuki, the moyo he gets in the continuation will really worry Black.

After the connection at 75, I was sure of winning. Even though I hardly had any secure territory, my intuition told me that it was impossible that Black be behind, with such good shape in the centre.

The kosumi-tsuke 77 and the hane 79 are a very severe response to 76.

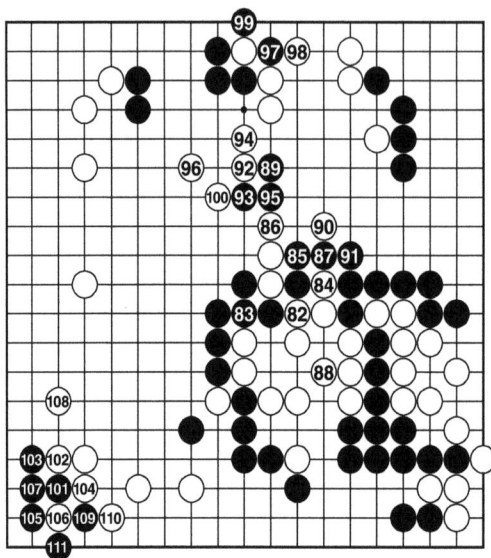

Figure 6 (82 – 111)

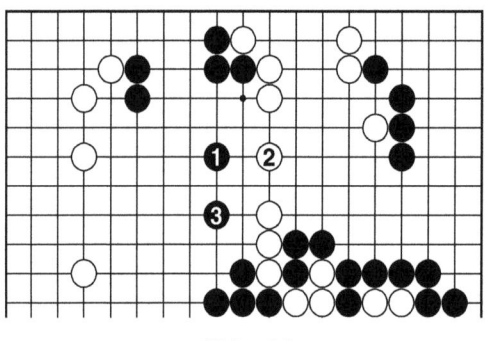

Dia. 14

Figure 6

I have the bad habit of becoming overly optimistic when I have the lead. Black 89 is a shameful move! The three white stones in the centre have little value.

Diagram 14

Simply playing 1 and 3 is better.

In the game, as I had decided to capture the three stones, White gets to play on the outside up to 96. The exchange of the three black stones 89, 93 and 95 for the three white stones at 92, 94 and 96 is obviously bad for Black. What is more, Black is obliged to capture 97 in gote.

The fact that I won, even with such bad moves, means that I really obtained an enormous lead at the beginning.

In this game, I was extremely concerned about grandeur; but at the end, I also played some horrible moves…

Result: White resigns.

Chapter 3

The cosmic style with White

So far, I have mostly commented my own games. My message is simple: it is not so important to learn joseki by heart or to make progress in your fuseki. What is essential is to truly love go.

Some may say: "You won't win your games if you don't have good technique."

But don't you agree that it is a shame to get upset simply over the result of a game?

Go is such an extraordinary game. Try to love it as much as possible, to love human beings and to love the Earth, our Earth. Such love brings freshness and richness to life.

To play luminous, shining moves, one must love the stones one plays with… Knowing books is not enough. Moves that really please you, stones played with love, can also move other people.

In this chapter, I present games where White adopts the cosmic style. However, in go, the colour – Black or White – makes little difference. As always, the strategy with the cosmic style is the same: one must move towards the centre.

Game 1: Territory? Who cares?

Even game played in 1968 between
Miyashita Shuyo 9-dan, Black, and
Takemiya Masaki 3-dan, White.

I would like to show you a game I played against Mr Miyashita Shuyo in the Pro Juketsu tournament in 1968, when I was ranked 3-dan.

The Pro Juketsu tournament doesn't take place any more, but I have some good memories of it. In 1968, I came eighth in the tournament, and then fifth the year after. People gave me the nickname 'Juketsu boy'[1].

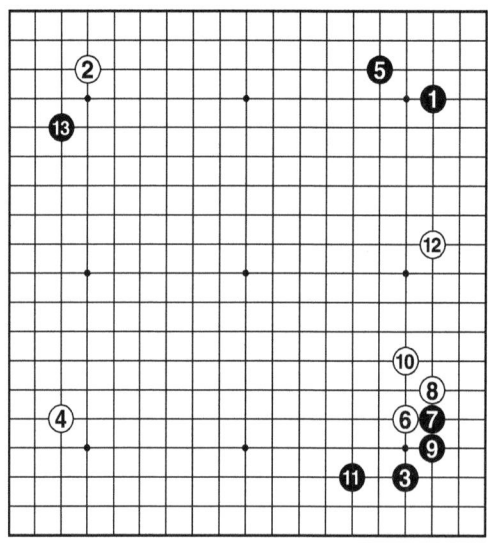

Figure 1 (1 – 13)

Figure 1

When I study my games from that period, I find that I played as I felt. Indeed, when my moyo strategy worked well, I played very well and took pleasure from my game. On the other hand, in the games I lost, my playing was extremely poor. The difference is quite clear.

I also believe I saw the goban with more purity than I do now. The young Takemiya would express all he felt on the goban.

---

[1] *The Juketsu tournament was a tournament for the top 10 professionals. Takemiya was only 17 in 1968. (Editor's note)*

The following game is a good example. While Mr Miyashita tries to make territory at all costs, my stones naturally move towards the centre. I played moves that pleased me.

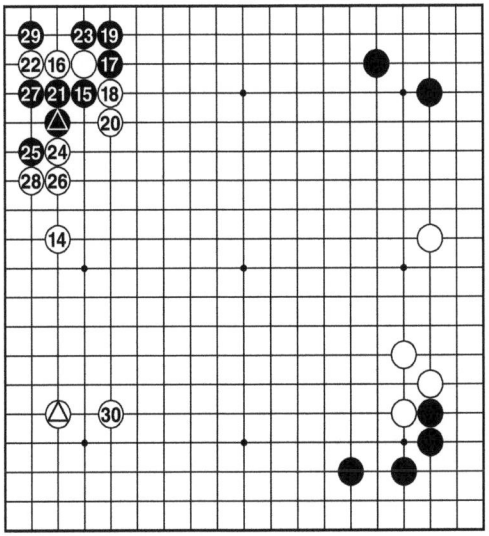

Figure 2   (14 – 30)

Figure 2

How should one answer Black's kakari 13 (⬤)?

In the game, White gains thickness with the sequence up to 28. White then makes a shimari with 30.

Apparently, the sequence in the top left corner is a joseki. But I don't care whether it is joseki or not. The sequence comes naturally through trying to make the most of the ⬭ marked stone.

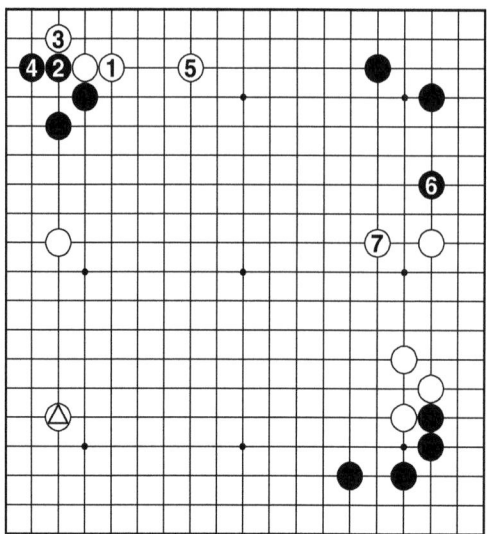

Dia. 1

Diagram 1

For example, one might be tempted to play this sequence in response to the kosumi-tsuke 15.

Black settles himself with 2 and 4, and then White plays tenuki and plays 5. This is a joseki. Next, Black takes a large point with 6 and White plays a tobi at 7. This is the usual joseki.

However, look closer: the stone ⓦ is not working at all.

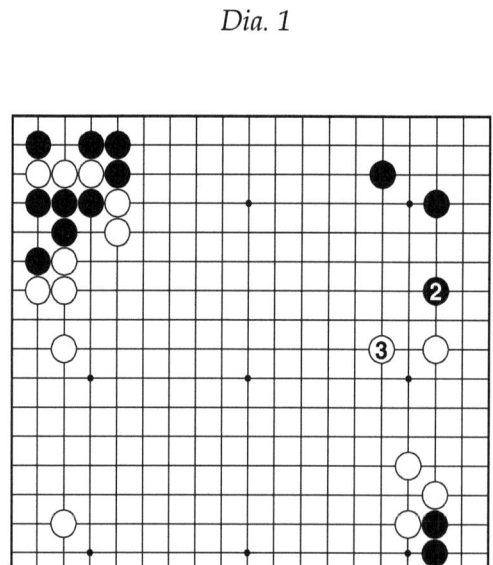

Dia. 2

Diagram 2

Similarly, for White 30, the usual shimari at 1 is not bad, but does it make White's thickness in the top left work fully?

Nonetheless, if you prefer Diagram 1 or 2, then do play as you feel.

You should play the moves that please you. Even so, it is still useful to listen to me a little; you might learn something.

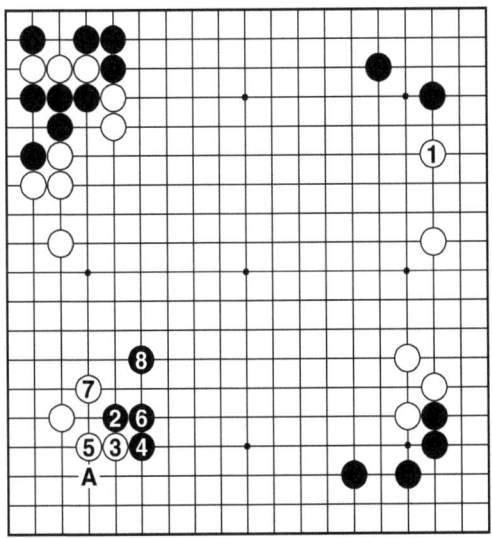

Dia. 3

Diagram 3

It is not good to make a hiraki (extension) with 1 instead of a shimari in the bottom left. The approach at 2 is unusual, but works very well in this position. White's influence is useless after 8.

If Black plays the kakari at A instead of 2, White is very happy to play the kake 3.

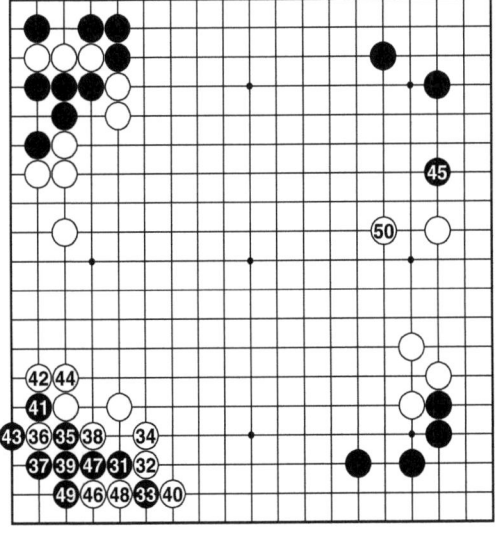

Figure 3 (31 – 50)

Figure 3

The fighting from 31 onwards is not a joseki. Some may find the sequence up to 44 overly complicated. In any case, no one can suggest a better variation. Anyway, you don't need to imitate what we professionals play.

One very important thing is certain: White must make the most of his central influence. White can play as he likes as long as he follows this principle.

As I have told you already, when you do not know where to play, ask yourself: "In what spirit should I play?" instead of "Where should I play?". Figure 3 is a typical example of this.

It is true that Black takes sente and gets to play 45, but White has a very agreeable yose sente sequence of 46 to 48 before playing the tobi at 50. White feels fine at this point.

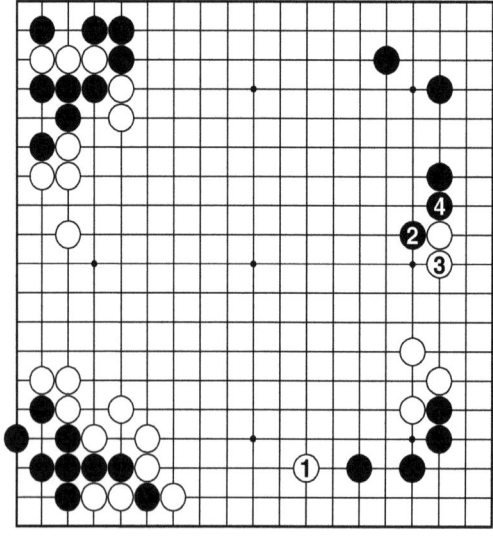

Dia. 4

Diagram 4

From a territorial point of view, one might take the large point at 1 (in this Diagram) instead of 50. However, I do not like Black 2 and 4 limiting my moyo.

It is true that the lower side is big, but one can have even bigger dreams for the centre. Compared with the limitless universe, the Earth – which seems big to us – is in fact very small. It is exactly the same here.

Figure 4

White 52 and 54: such calm!

White does not try to make territory. Some players may wonder how White can win with such moves. The answer is that territory will come by itself later. Believe me, now is not the time to make territory.

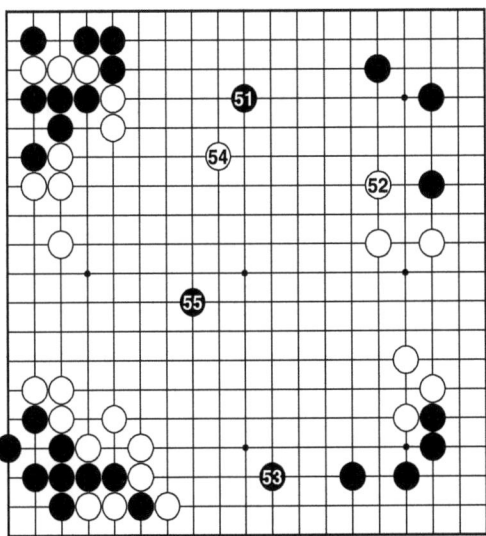

Figure 4 (51 – 55)

Diagram 5

One professional suggested playing 54 somewhere around 1 in this Diagram. Perhaps this does work better and is more usual. But in a position like this, I will always play a move like 54.

I cannot give you the precise reason why.

My intuition simply says to me: "White 1 is rather small. Let us develop the moyo to its fullest with 54."

Of course, Black has to invade the moyo, but I did not expect such a deep invasion as 55. This move illustrates well Mr Miyashita's character; he was sometimes called 'the raging bull'. He tries to completely destroy my moyo with his famous fighting strength.

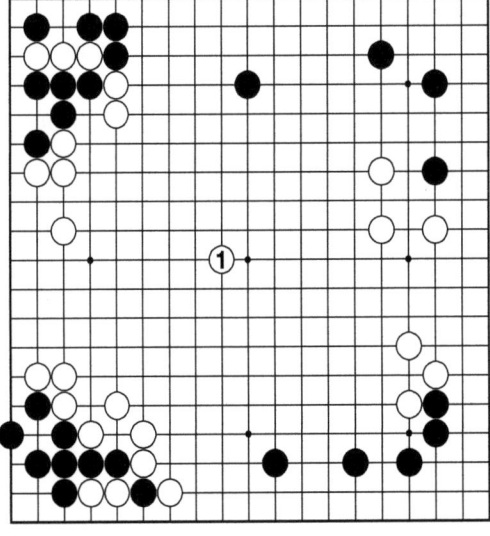

Dia. 5

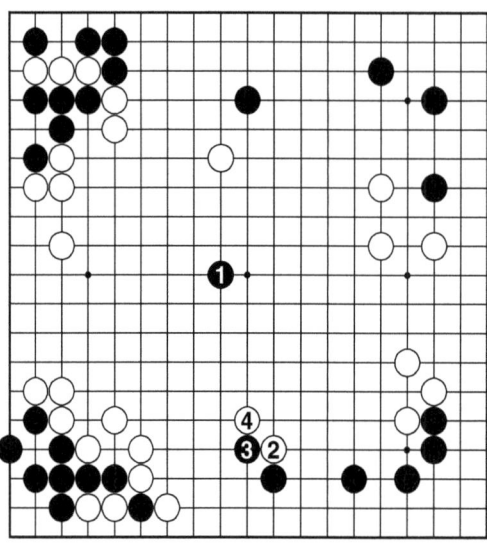

Dia. 6

Diagram 6

Black would usually play another move, like 1 in this Diagram. In this case, it does not seem as if a direct attack will work, so White can attack the central invading stone from a distance by pressing with 2 and 4.

In the game, how should White answer the deep invasion at 55? The answer is not very hard.

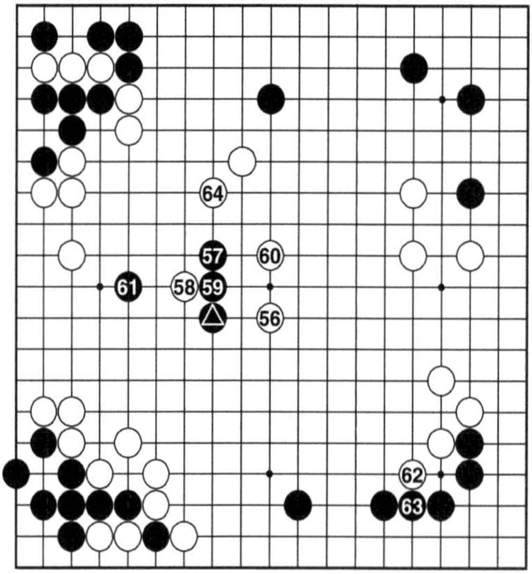

Figure 5

At a glance, we can see that the ● stone is too deep. One should attack with the boshi 56: this idea is very simple, and so, very good.

Figure 5 (56 – 64)

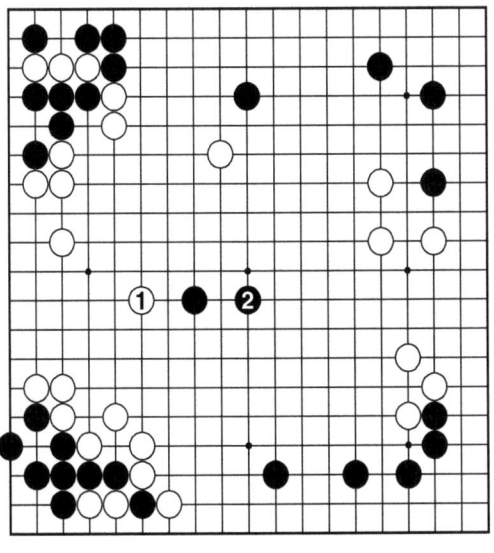

Dia. 7

Diagram 7

Some may prefer to make territory with 1 instead of 56. The cosmic style is undoubtedly not for them. What is the point of the influence White has constructed if he lets Black escape with 2?

Influence is useless if you immediately try to use it to make territory.

On the contrary, influence is precious when used to attack, not to make territory. The truth is that if you attack, your territory will come easily of itself.

With my attack at 58 and 60, the game is promising for me. However, I made errors attacking later on, and in the end I lost the game.

Result: White resigns.

Game 2: Let's play moves that shine

Even game played in 1974 between
Rin Kaiho 9-dan, Black, and
Takemiya Masaki 7-dan, White.

Even with White, the cosmic style is based on the centre. Perhaps you think that the cosmic style does not work well for White? I answer that it matters little whether you are Black or White; colour is not at all important. This was clear in the previous game.

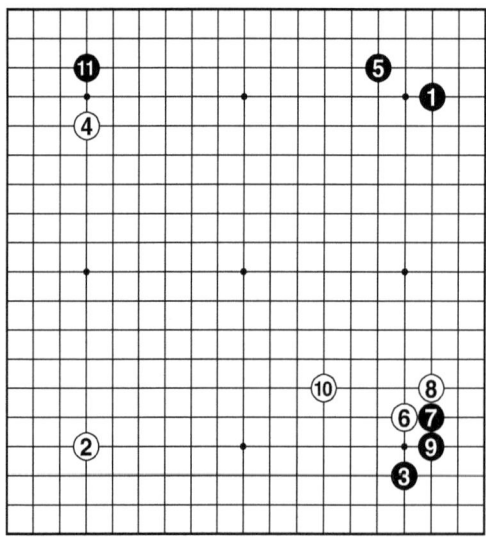

Figure 1 (1 – 11)

Figure 1

White 10 is a move that is in fashion at the moment, but around the time I played this game, it was a move I already knew.

Black plays tenuki and approaches the top left corner with 11.

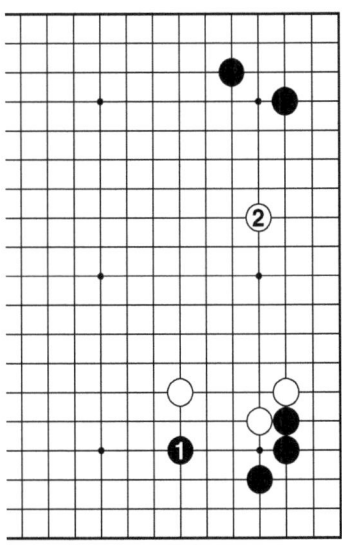

Dia. 1

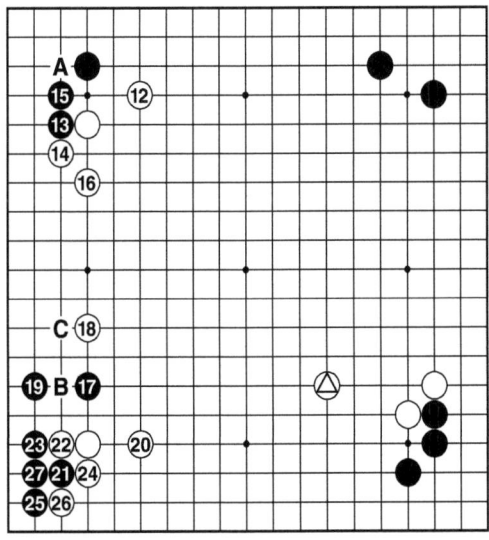

Figure 2　(12 – 27)

Diagram 1

If Black were to answer at 1, I would probably play 2 to develop my moyo.

Black 10 of the game is one of my favourite moves: it shines out simultaneously towards the centre and the side.

Figure 2

After the marked white ⊘ stone has been played, my strategy is clear: I must make this stone work at its fullest.

Therefore 12 is a natural move. For instance, claiming territory with the tsuke at A is not very good. The ⊘ stone in the centre loses its value.

When White chooses to make outside influence with 12, I think you will agree that the ⊘ stone starts to shine brightly.

Move 17 also takes into account the ⊘ stone.

Were Black to play the usual kakari at B, White would play the pincer at C. This is why Black chose the kakari at 17. Given White, what would you play after 17?

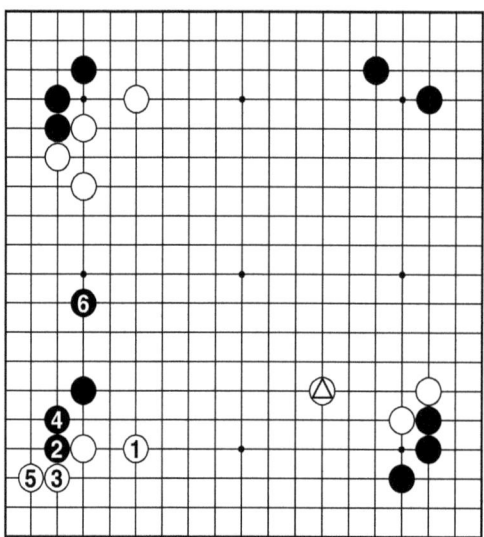

Dia. 2

Diagram 2

If your reaction is: "Playing 1 as in the joseki can't be bad", you don't yet grasp this game.

Do you realise what has happened when Black settles himself with 2 to 6? Not only has White's influence in the top left been wiped out, but also the ⊘ stone is much less effective.

If you want to play in this manner, then be consistent and make territory right from the beginning. To each their own.

If, on the contrary, you appreciate the beauty of stones directed towards the centre, I would like you to make the pincer at 18. This makes White's stones work at their fullest.

Diagram 3

The tobis 1 and 3 fall into the trap. The three Black stones will come under attack.

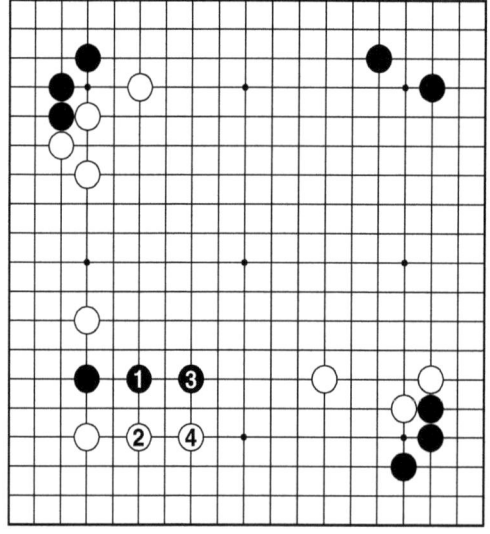

Dia. 3

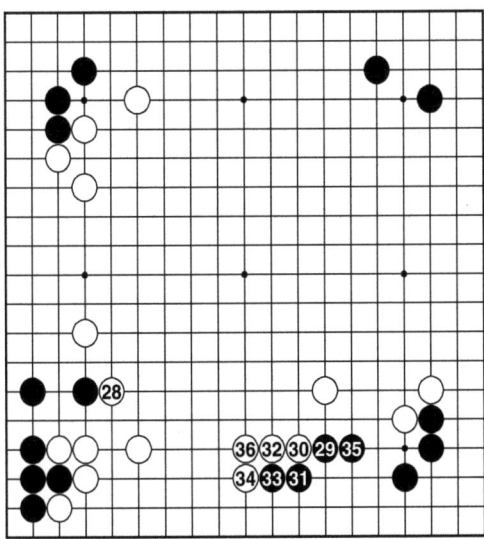

Figure 3 (28 – 36)

Figure 3

White is quite happy enough to shut Black into the corner. However, 28 is a mistake.

I felt fine closing in the Black group but, looking closely, we see that this lets Black take the very important point 29. This interferes with White's influence.

Diagram 4

I should have exchanged 1 for 2 and only then played 3. White's influence works well in this variation. My game still needed fine tuning.

Black could play 2 at A but this is perhaps not very good for him, as the white sagari at 2 is very severe. This leaves a lot of aji in the corner.

With only one error, 28, the game becomes difficult for White. This is the problem with moyo games. Stones that shined like diamonds up to 28 are changed into leaden marbles.

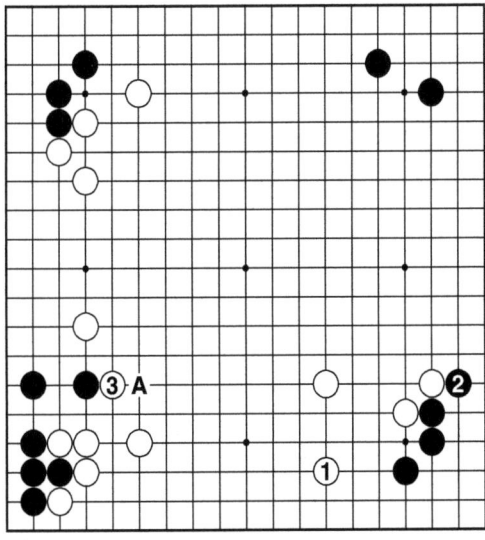

Dia. 4

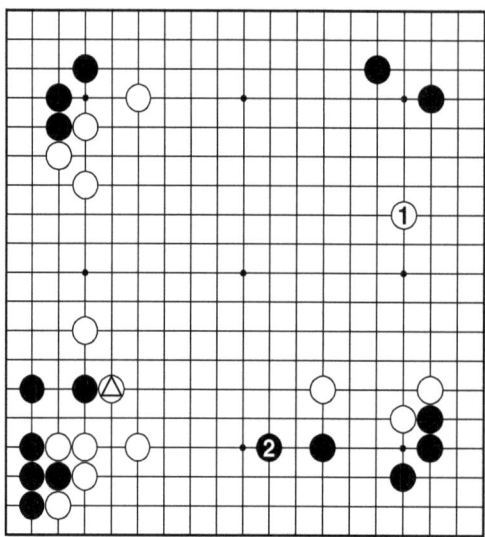

Dia. 5

As you know, I like stones that are directed towards the centre, but this is not true in all situations. For instance, up to 28 in this game I gain influence. But once Black has occupied the very important point 29, the stone at 28 loses its value. I do not like this.

Moves 30 to 36 were played to minimize the effect of this mistake.

Diagram 5

Of course, I would like to make the extension of 1, but the ⓐ stone loses all its value if Black gets to play the tobi 2. This would be intolerable.

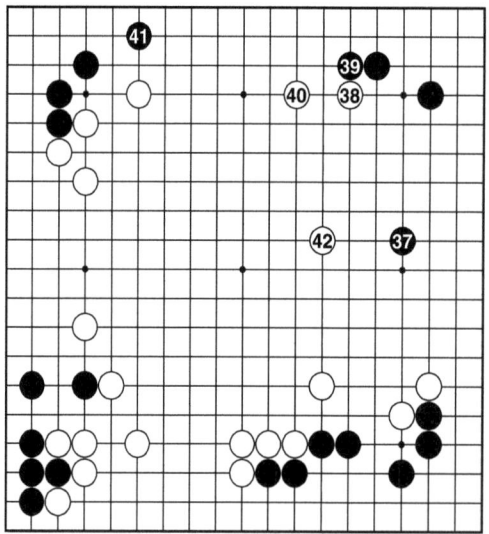

Figure 4 (37 – 42)

Figure 4

Move 37 is very good for Black. Frankly, this is a difficult game for White.

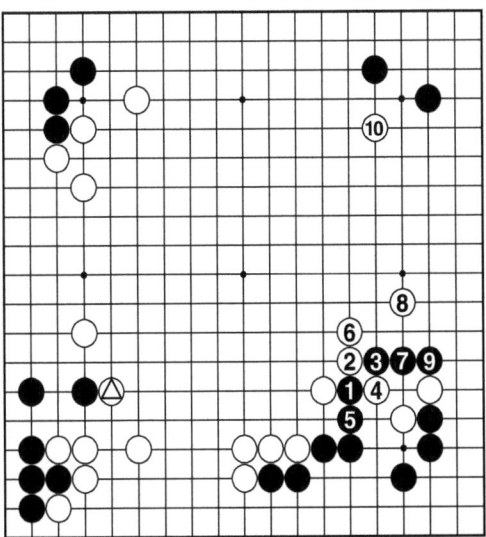

Dia. 6

Diagram 6

White is waiting for Black to try to capture the two white stones in the bottom right. White sacrifices some useless stones with 4 to 8, and then plays at 10. Black enlarges his territory a little, but the influence gained by White is much more important. In this Diagram, the stone ⊘ works well – in fact every single white stone is working well.

As the position was tough for Black, I decided to play 38 and 40. The idea is to give life to this game by developing my moyo to its utmost.

Diagram 7

White could have simply played 1. If Black plays 2, the kake at 3 isn't bad. But I preferred to develop my moyo as much as possible.

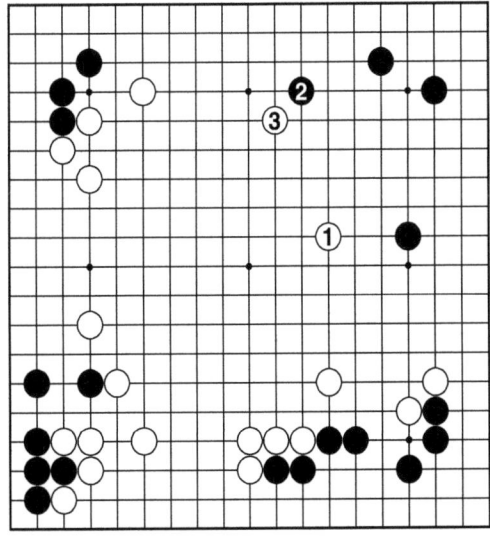

Dia. 7

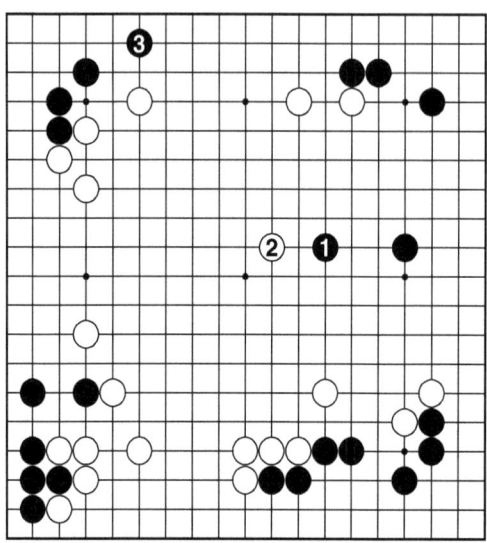

Dia. 8

Diagram 8

In the game, 41 is a move that is too territorial. The vital point of this game is the tobi at 1 in this Diagram. White answers at 2, but his moyo is smaller than in the figure.

When White takes the vital point with 42, the game becomes more even.

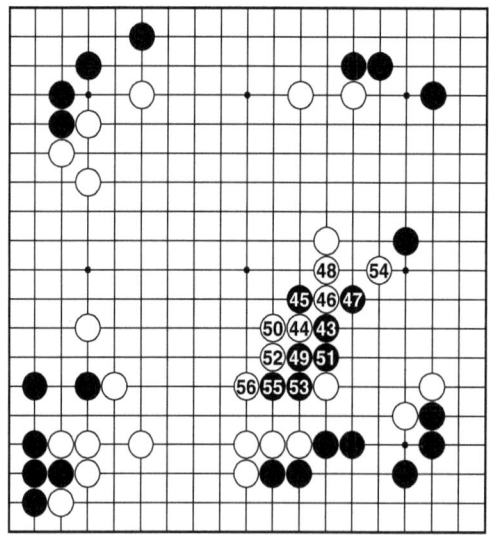

Figure 5 (43 – 56)

Figure 5

Black reduces White's moyo with 43, and White stops Black's advance with 44 to 56.

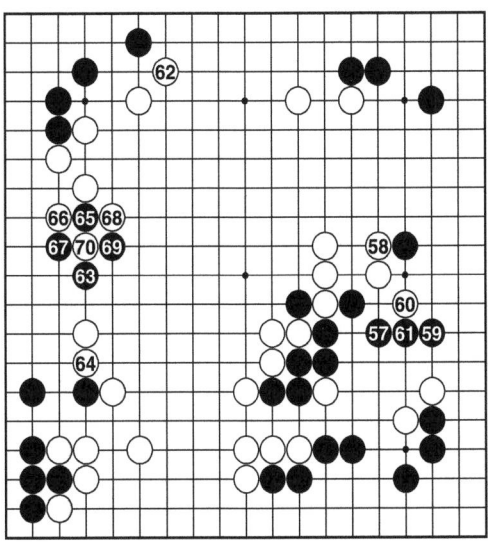

Figure 6 (57 – 70)

Figure 6

Black invades with 63, uchikomi. White cannot easily capture this stone. Do you think that White will lose if this stone manages to live? That would be sad! It's better to focus on making profit through attacking this stone. That way one feels much more at ease.

White defends at 64 and then Black starts a ko with the tesuji combination of 65 to 69.

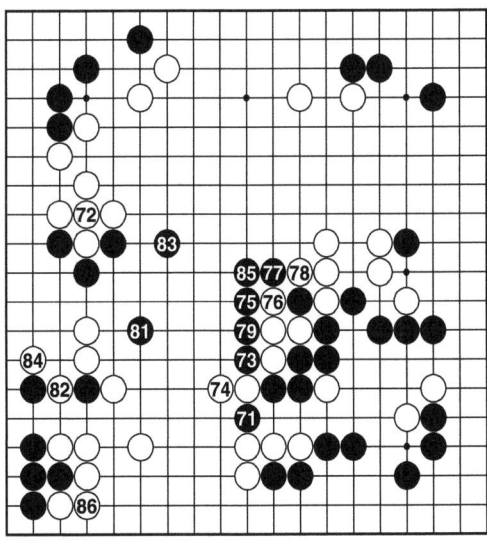

Figure 7 (71 – 86)
80 at 78

Figure 7

Next, Black makes a ko threat with 71, and White connects the ko with 72. With the moves up to 86, the surprise result is that White gets the corner in compensation for Black's invasion of the centre.

The centre, which was very important for White, has been totally destroyed. We can see that the game is very close. As the Black group in the centre is not completely alive, White probably has a slight edge.

This game concluded with Black resigning, but the result is not important.

At the beginning of the game, it is enough to just play moves that shine. Even we professionals, who depend upon tournaments, think that the result is secondary and that the content of the game is essential. What is difficult about losing is that I do not like disappointing my supporters...

I hope that you get pleasure from go without being obsessed by the result. At least once, in each of your games, do please try to contemplate the goban. Try to use your intuition to find shining moves. You may very well discover something.

Result: Black resigns.

Game 3: Do not miss the tennôzan[1]

Even game played in 1980 between
Rin Kaiho 9-dan, Black, and
Takemiya Masaki 9-dan, White.

Intuition is all-important in moyo games. Without meaning to seem proud, let me say that I hardly thought at all during this fuseki. I trusted only in my intuition.

The tennôzan was crucial in this game. A tennôzan often appears in large moyo games. Once again: it is a question of feeling, and not of reading.

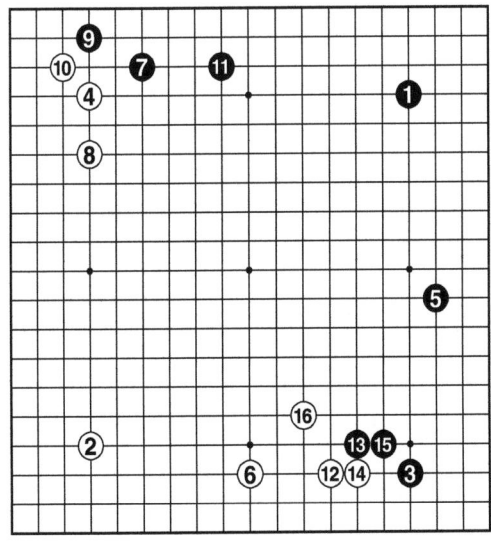

Figure 1

Early on, a tennôzan appears: at White 16. Why does White play this keima, when there are so many other interesting points on the goban?

Figure 1 (1 – 16)

[1] *See the explanation of this term on page 30 (Translator's note).*

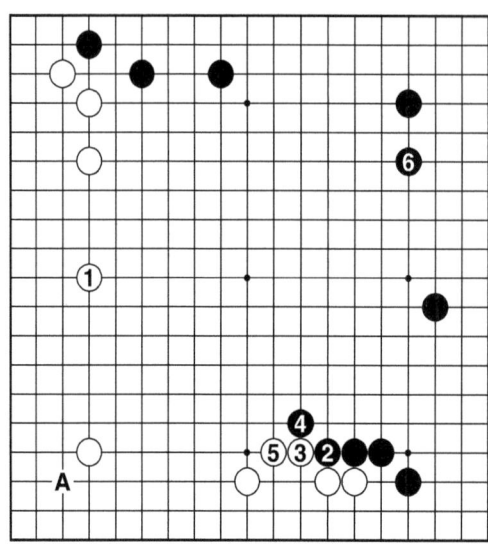

Dia. 1

Diagram 1

For instance, White could make a sanrensei with 1. Then Black would very happily play the sequence 2 to 5.

Compare this with the figure: both players' moyos have changed considerably.

Next, Black would make a shimari with 6, developing his large moyo. Also, the san-san at A in the bottom left corner is still open. Black would be very pleased with this fuseki.

A tennôzan like 16 has nothing to do with precise moves such as tesuji or yose; one cannot find the tennôzan through calculation.

So, one needs intuition – but how does one gain such intuition?

One method is to study professional games. Getting teaching from strong players is also useful, but I think that your heart is the most important factor.

If you play with your heart, the very same heart that is moved by music or films, you will understand the beauty of go.

In go, one neither needs deep reading nor a psychological strategy. It is your heart, beating in tune with the world's beauty, which is essential. I believe this very strongly.

If everybody had a heart like this, war would no longer exist.

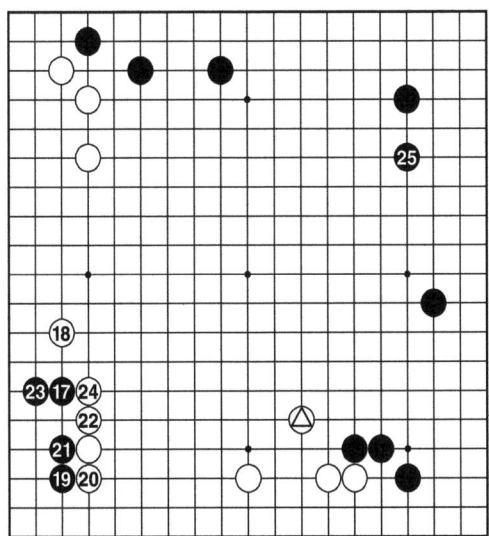

Figure 2 (17 – 25)

Figure 2

Black would be in trouble were both sides to continue developing their moyo, because White has taken the tennôzan ⬙. So Black plays the kakari 17. White then pincers and continues to build his moyo.

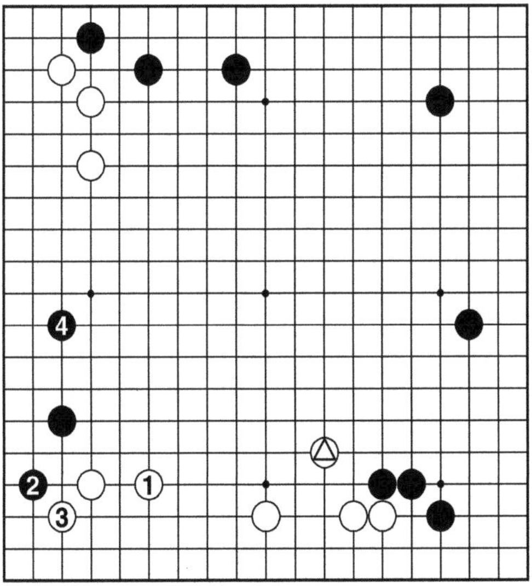

Diagram 2

White 1, instead of 18, is not bad. But it does not feel right to me: Black has established himself too easily in my moyo.

In the game, taking the san-san immediately after the pincer at 18 is the normal move.

With 20 to 24, White's outside influence increases, and the stone ⬙ begins to shine brightly.

Dia. 2

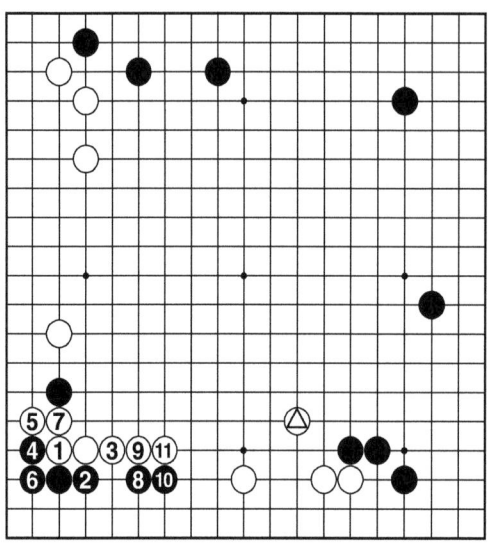

Dia. 3

Diagram 3

Instead of playing White 20, some players prefer to block on the other side, at 1 in this Diagram. This gives a different game, but here the ⊘ stone is not very brilliant, whereas in the game it shines very brightly.

The more one is aware of such differences, the more interesting go becomes.

Back to the game: the shimari at 25 is big. Now try to find the next move...

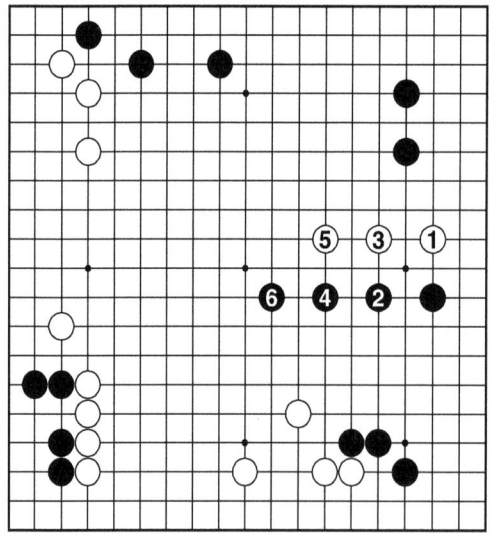

Dia. 4

Diagram 4

First, here is a bad choice. In fact, the worst idea is to invade at 1. Black plays three consecutive tobi, 2 to 6, and White's moyo is completely destroyed.

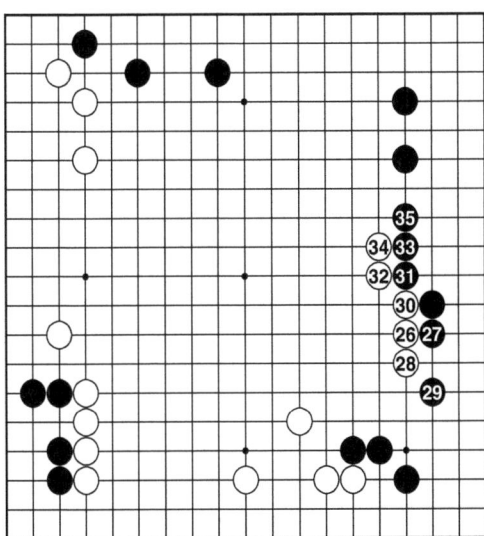

Figure 3 (26 – 35)

Figure 3

White's central moyo is more important than the right side. One must therefore play moves which do not damage the moyo, for instance 26.

The sequence up to 35 is normal. Black makes territory on the right side; but look closely and you will see that the gain is rather small. On the other hand, White has an enormous central moyo.

Even so, I was not very experienced: I next played a very slow move.

However, before that I have a remark to make about Black 27.

Diagram 5

If Black pushes with 1 and 3 and then plays the keima 5, the white magari 6 becomes a very good move – it is in fact another tennôzan.

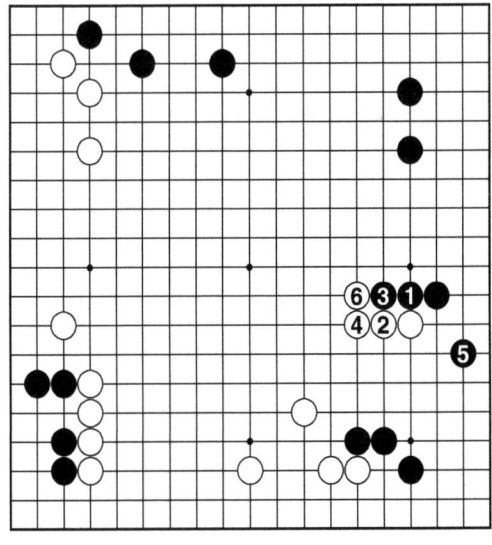

Dia. 5

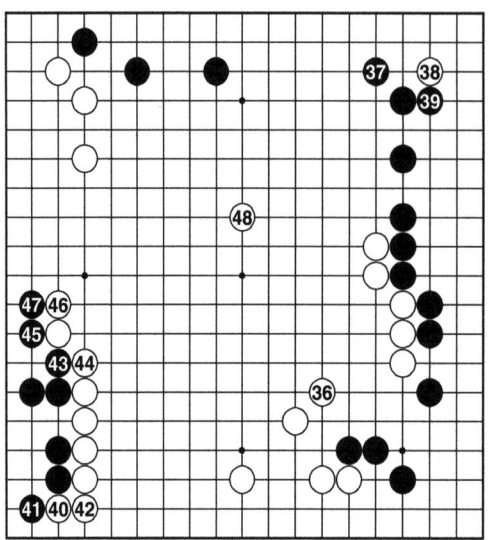

Figure 4 (36 – 48)

Figure 4

I next played a bad move: White 36 is very slow.

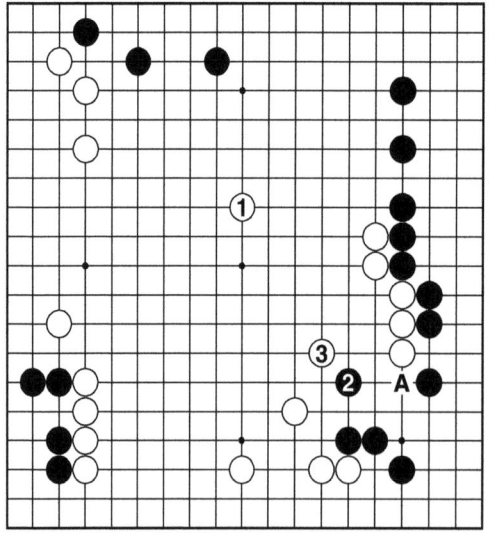

Dia. 6

Diagram 6

Why didn't I think of playing at the tennôzan, White 1 in this Diagram? A white move at A on the right side is sente, so Black cannot go any further than 2. White would then stop him with 3. There is nothing at all bothersome here.

However, Mr Rin was kind here: he gave me another chance to take the tennôzan by playing 37.

Finally, White gets to take the tennôzan with 48.

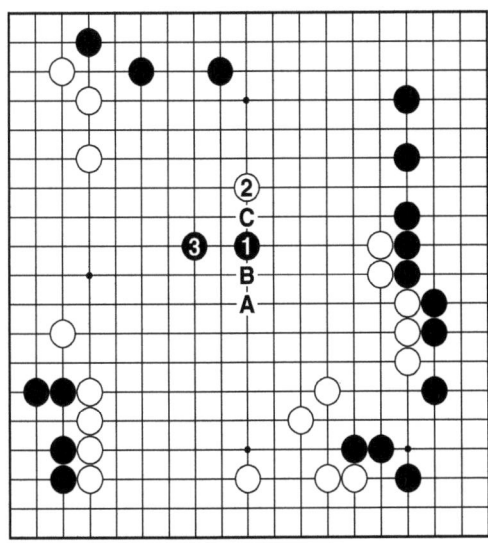

Dia. 7

Diagram 7

Surely Black must play at 1. If White answers at 2, Black plays a tobi at 3 and his group cannot be killed, while answering at A is not enough for White.

Black 1 is finely placed: if Black plays B, White would play the boshi at C; this would be dangerous for Black.

Black 47 is another move that is beside the point: it should be played in the centre.

Although I have entitled this game 'Don't miss the tennôzan', in fact, I show you a game where both players miss the tennôzan!

Professionals are also human beings. Depending on their mental and physical state, they can also play horrible moves. This is another reason why go is so interesting – or perhaps this is just an excuse!

Result: Black resigns.

Game 4: Dancing in the sky

Even game played in 1985 between
Yamashiro Hiroshi, 9-dan, Black, and
Takemiya Masaki, Honinbo, White.

Figure 1

It is said that fuseki plays should mostly be on the third and fourth lines. However, I advise you not to believe this. Let me show you a game where I played a very unusual move.

The tobi at 10 reflects my character: I like taking my time.

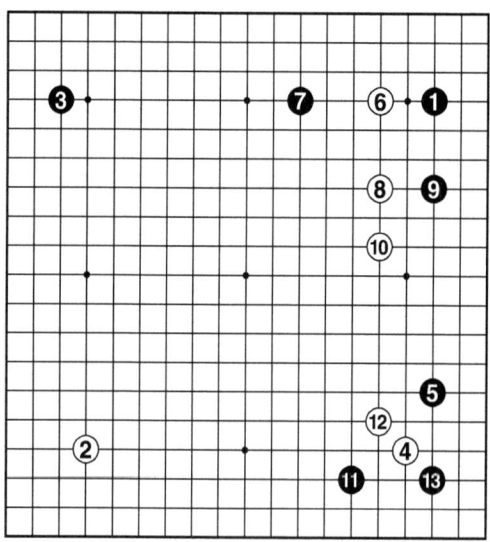

Figure 1 (1 – 13)

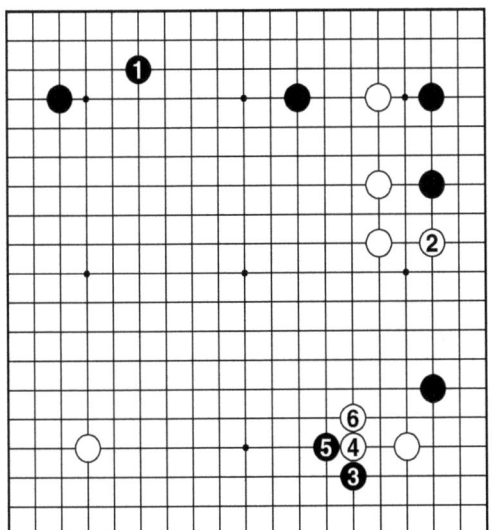

Dia. 1

Diagram 1

If Black plays 11 at 1, then White 2 is just as good as Black's shimari.

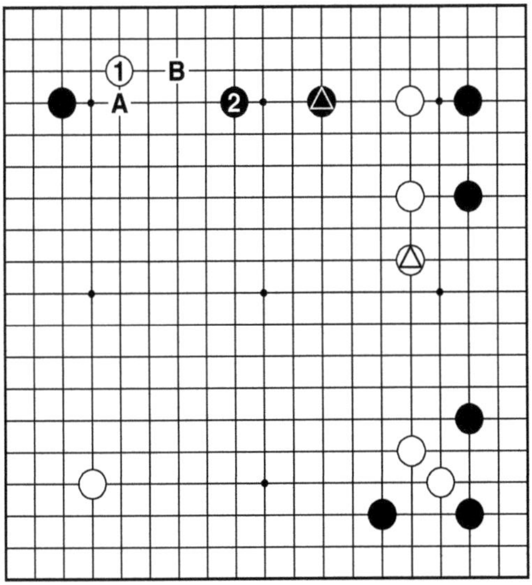

Diagram 2

Now, we come to the following problem: White could approach at 1, but then Black has a pincer attack at 2. The tobi ⬠ aims at attacking the ⬠ stone, but Black gets to take the initiative with 2.

White could play 1 at A, but then Black pincers at B.

Dia. 2

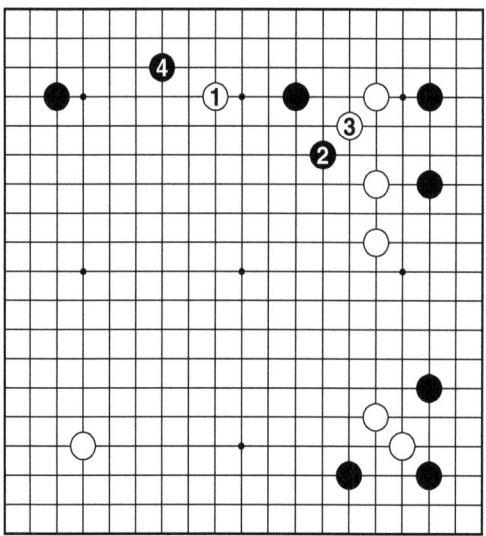

Dia. 3

Diagram 3

How about the pincer at 1?

If Black plays a kikashi at 2, and then follows up with a pincer at 4, the result is not clear.

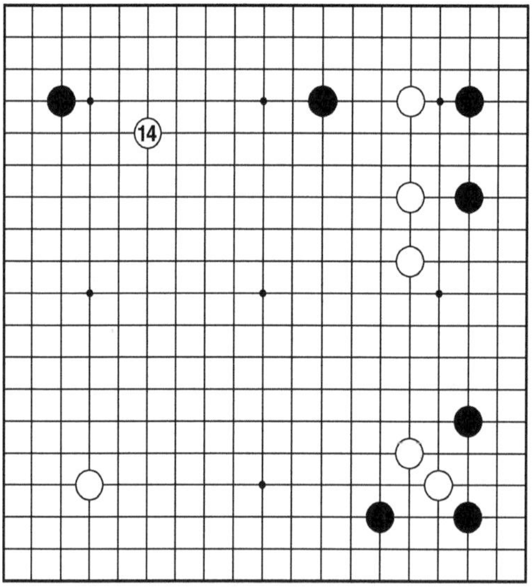

Figure 2 (14)

Figure 2

Now we have a surprise move: White 14!

What sort of move is this? Although it may seem strange, it felt natural at the time.

The idea is that there is no good pincer to attack this stone with.

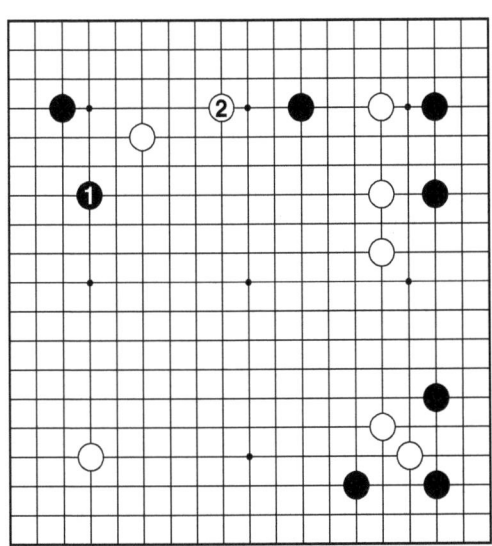

Dia. 4

Diagram 4

If Black answers at 1, White can pincer at 2.

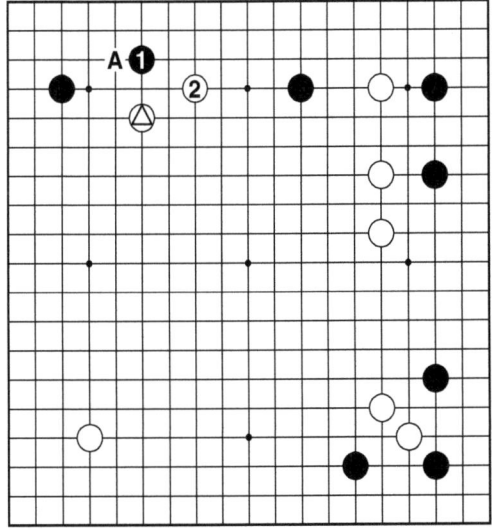

Dia. 5

Diagram 5

What happens if Black plays like this?

To be honest, White 14 comes more from my intuition than from my reading of sequences. I don't know exactly how one should play, but I would probably play the keima 2 to build influence. White then has good follow-ups with the tsuke at A and an attack on the ⊘ stone.

What do you think of White 14?

Who decreed that the fuseki is based on the third and fourth lines? Do not believe in 'common sense'.

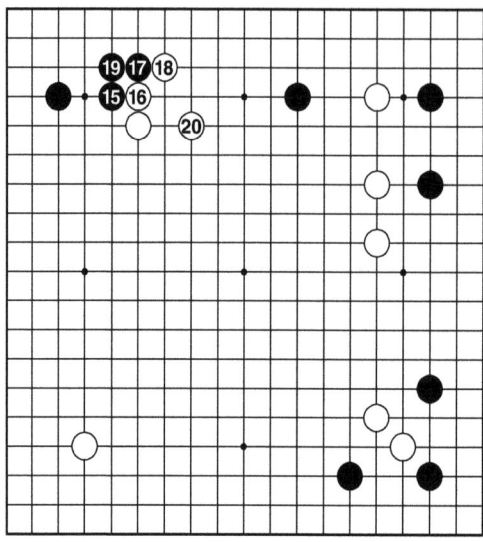

Figure 3 (15 – 20)

Figure 3

Mr Yamashiro answered with 15. After 16, Black is happy enough to make territory with the hane-tsugi 17 to 19. On the other hand, I'm also happy to make a good shape, with the moves up to 20.

White 20 is also a move that reflects my character.

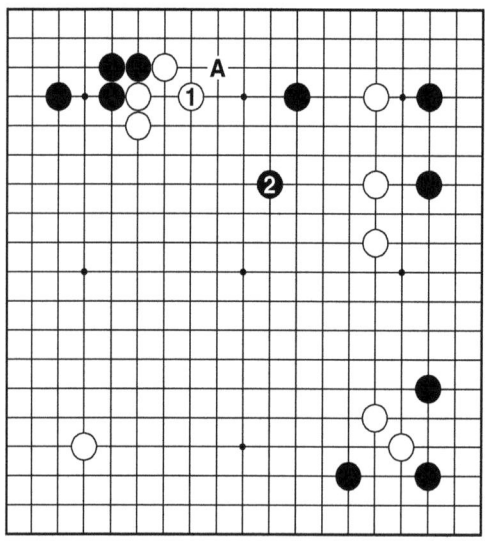

Dia. 6

Diagram 6

White loses fewer points in the yose with 1. But Black would still play 2, as in the game. The problem is that the key point A is still open.

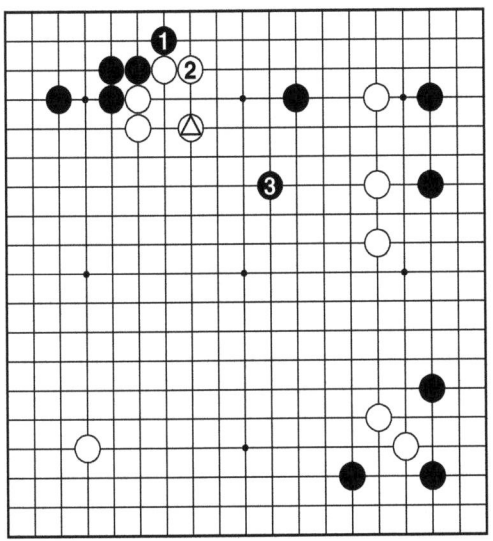

Dia. 7

Diagram 7

The advantage of White 20 (⊘) is that even if Black later plays the hane 1, White makes a good shape with 2.

Since in any case this game will lead to a battle in the centre, it is better to prepare for the fighting instead of thinking about territory.

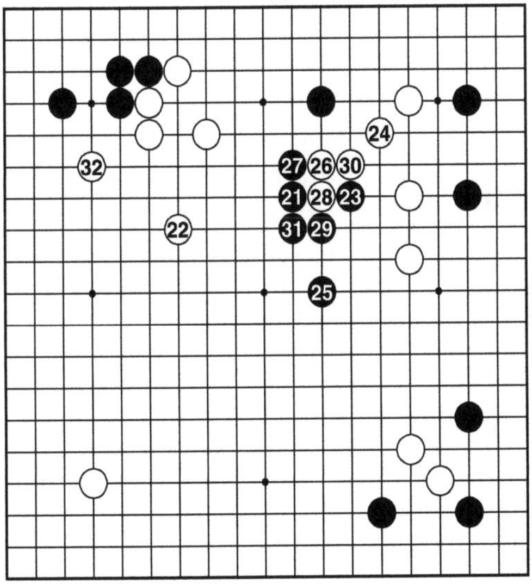

Figure 4 (21 – 32)

Figure 4

Black moves towards the centre with 21. So does White with 22. Black tries to make shape with 23 to 25; I try to stop him with the nozoki (peep) at 26. White reinforces his group with 32; I find that this is not a bad fuseki for White.

I would like to make a remark about the combat on the top side.

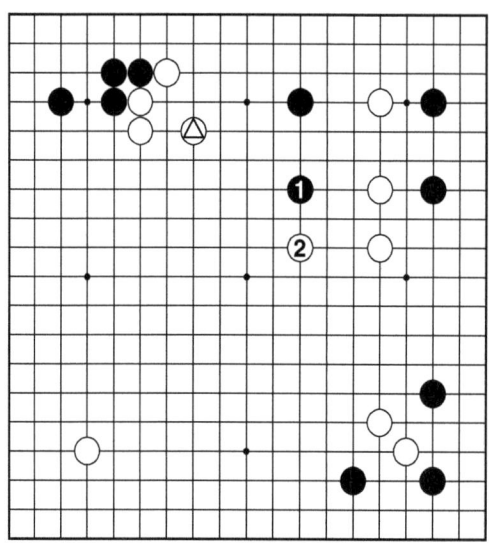

Dia. 8

Diagram 8

Due to the ⊘ stone, the niken-tobi 1 is not ideal, as White has a good answer at 2. In this position all of White's stones are working fully. Clearly this is favourable for White.

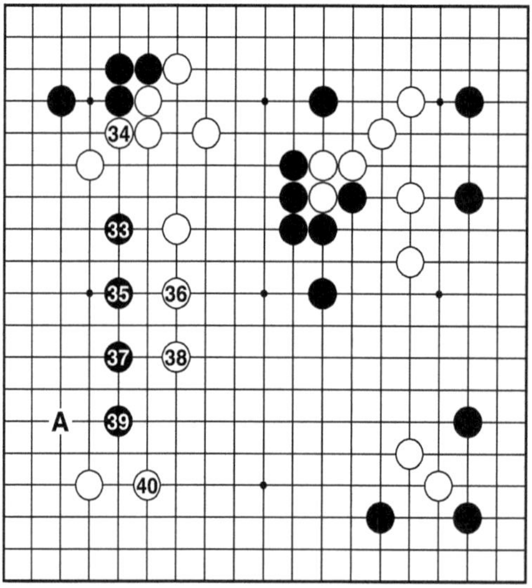

Figure 5 (33 – 40)

Figure 5

Black 33 is too severe, and lets White take the initiative. Playing 33 at A would be normal.

Each player plays several tobi up to White 40; and after 40, Black has two weak groups.

If there is to be a battle in the centre, all of White's stones are ready.

By the way, have you noticed that while Black has made quite a lot of territory, White doesn't have any!

I have already told you: it is not necessary to try to make territory. The beginning of a game is like the early years in life. If you only think of money (territory) in this important period, you will never succeed in life.

At the beginning of a game, it is important to make influence to prepare for the battles to come. Territory will come naturally later on – a Japanese proverb says "power attracts money".

Figure 6

After the resolute move of Black 41, White cuts with 42–44. Now is perhaps the time to convert influence into territory. Black has to play 45 to 49 to stabilise his group, then White makes a large territory with 50 and 52. Such is the power of influence.

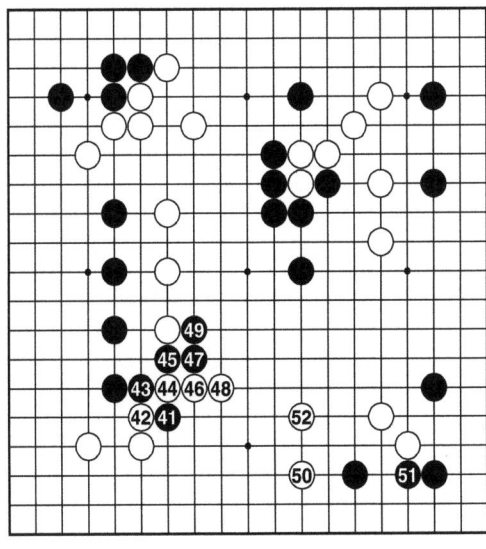

Now, what do you think of White 14 in Figure 2 (page 124)? It's like a stone thrown into the cosmos. According to how one plays, a simple stone can be transformed into a diamond. Isn't this amazing?

Figure 6 (41 – 52)

Result: In the end, White wins by 4½ points.

Game 5: A two-fold large moyo

Even game played in 1993 between
Otake Hideo 9-dan, Black, and
Takemiya Masaki, Judan, White.

Like me, Mr Otake's style favours influence. Still, my stones go further than his when we play together.

I am rather happy with the following game. I won it through influence. This game is quite typical of the cosmic style with White.

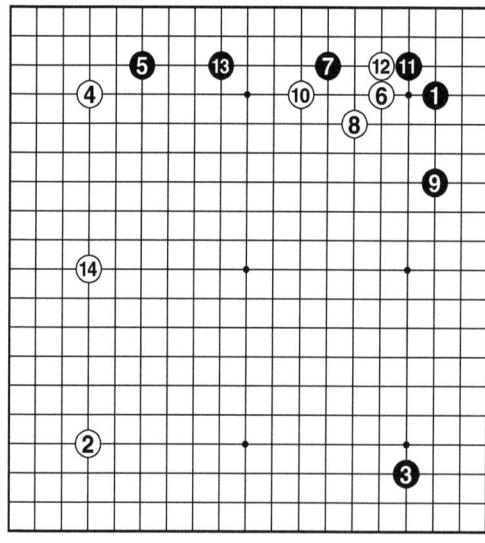

Figure 1

I almost always play on the hoshi, whether I be Black or White. Perhaps this means that my opponents can easily prepare their strategies against me. In fact, the beginning of this game is exactly the same as in a game we played one month earlier, in the Meijin.

Figure 1   (1 – 14)

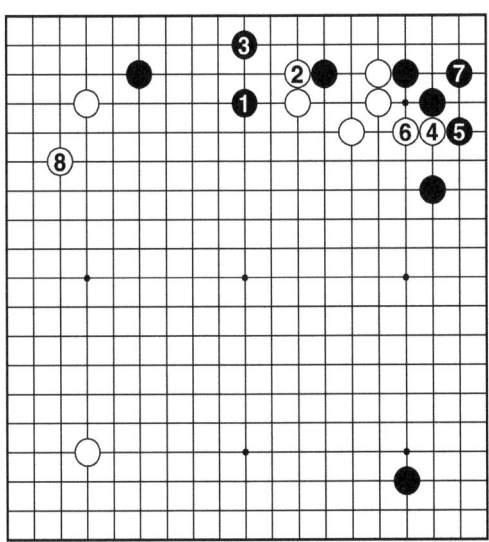

Dia. 1

Diagram 1

In that game, Mr Otake had played the moves 1 and 3. This time, he calmly played 13, niken-biraki. We are in the realms of intuition; there are many different possibilities. I decided to tenuki and take another hoshi with 14.

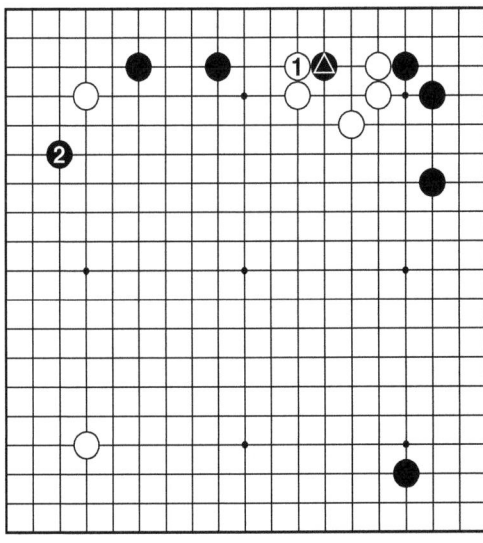

Dia. 2

Diagram 2

Some players probably find it necessary to capture the ▲ stone with 1, but this lets Black take the initiative with the pincer at 2.

Looking at the overall situation, it is clear that playing at 14 is much more important.

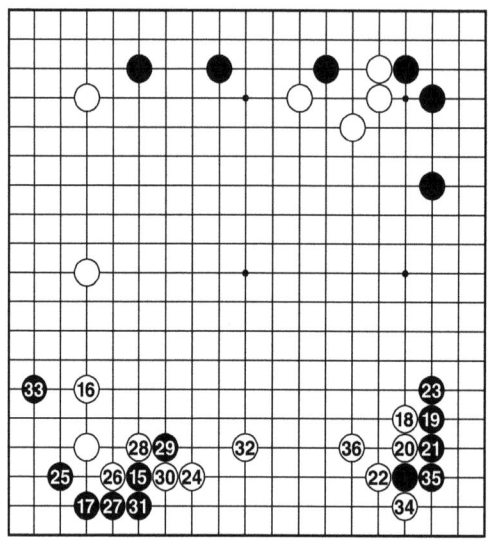

Figure 2 (15 – 36)

Figure 2

After the keima 17, the tenuki at 18 and the nadare (avalanche) plays, 20 to 22 were the fruit of deep reflection. With the pincer at 24, White creates a large moyo.

Black could have played 19 at 36 to prevent the birth of this moyo. Trying to make territory against the cosmic style really shows his fighting spirit.

The following Diagram shows the worst way for White to play.

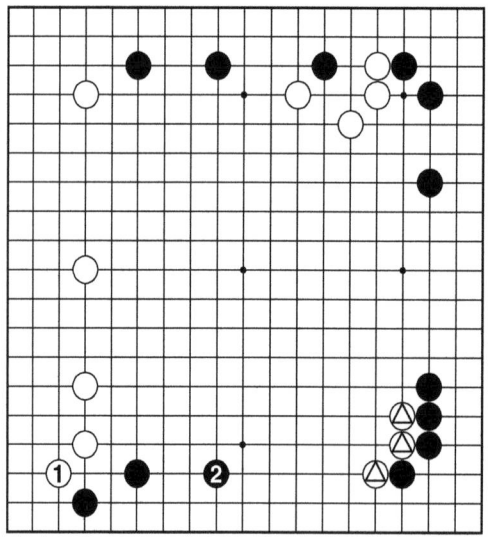

Dia. 3

Diagram 3

If White plays 24 at 1, Black is very happy to make an extension with 2. The three ⬿ stones, which have just been played, are then badly placed.

If you really want to play 1, don't play the avalanche in the first place.

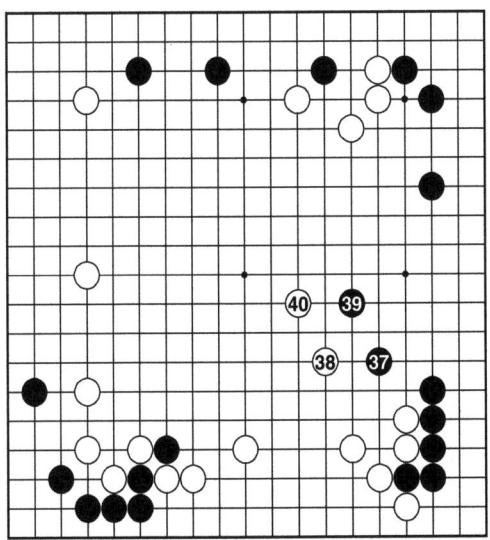

Figure 3 (37 – 40)

Figure 3

White 38 and 40 are the only possible responses to 37 and 39.

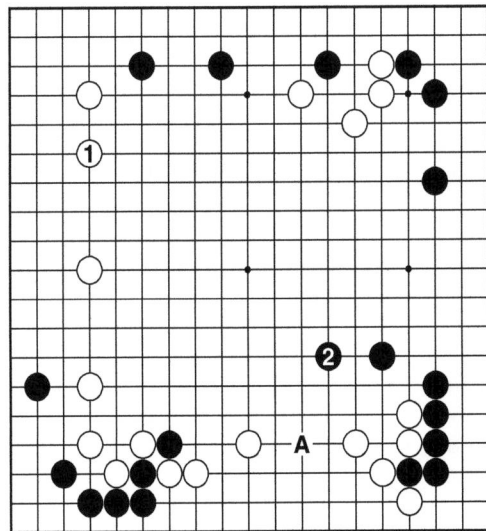

Dia. 4

Diagram 4

For instance, if White plays 1, Black plays the tobi 2 without hesitation. This nips in the bud any hopes White may have for a moyo on the lower side. Also, White's weakness at A becomes very worrisome.

A moyo game is practically over if one misses such a vital point. One has to work without cease to hone one's intuition.

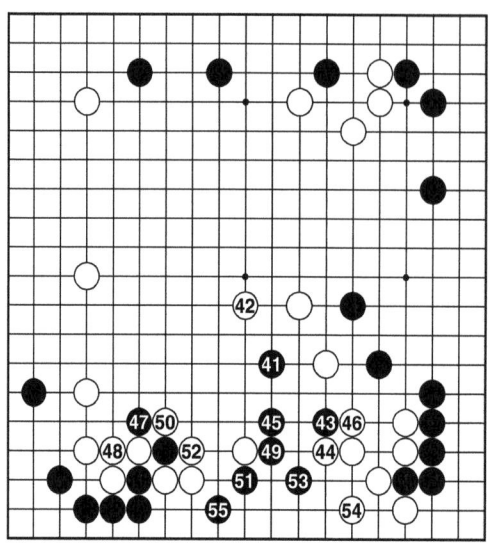

Figure 4

Black 41: what a deep invasion! Black wants to completely invade White's moyo.

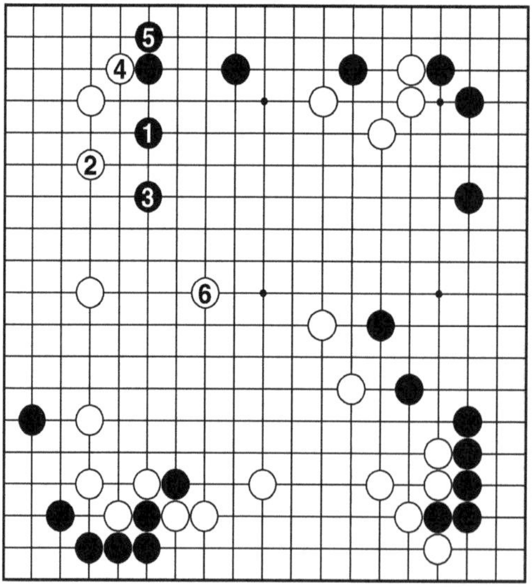

Figure 4 (41 – 45)

Diagram 5

The two tobi 1 and 3 are a natural idea. Still, White will probably get a large territory on the lower side. Perhaps this is why Black chose the risky invasion.

How should White deal with the invasion at 41?

Dia. 5

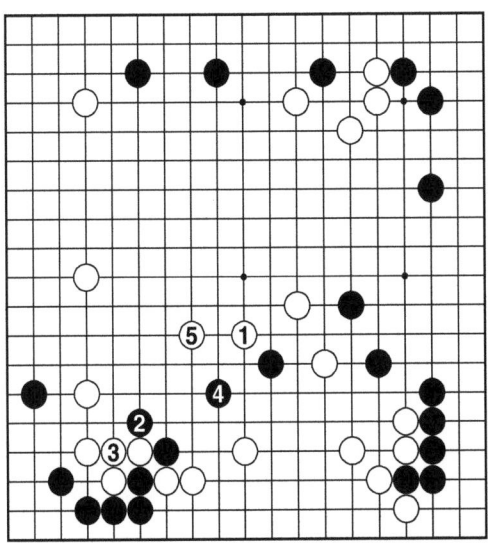

Dia. 6

Diagram 6

The keima 1 is very severe, and perfectly feasible. However, I don't know whether or not White can capture the stone at 41.

I chose a simple response: the tobi 42. Simple, normal moves are generally good enough in go.

The result is that Black easily lives and White's moyo has completely disappeared. Many players will suppose that White is very behind in the game.

However there is still hope...

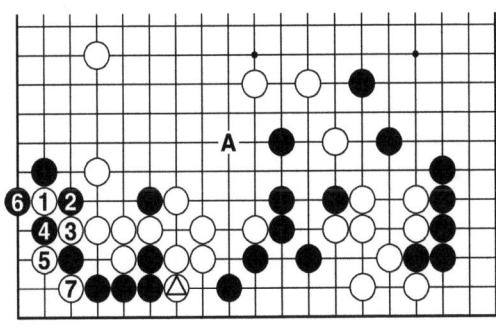

Dia. 7

White also has another plan...

Diagram 7

If White blocks with ⬤ he has a large yose sequence (1 to 7). If Black adds a move in the corner (for instance at 2) then we can say that ⬤ separates the two Black groups in sente. What is more, the Black group on the right is not completely alive: at the very least, White has a sente move at A.

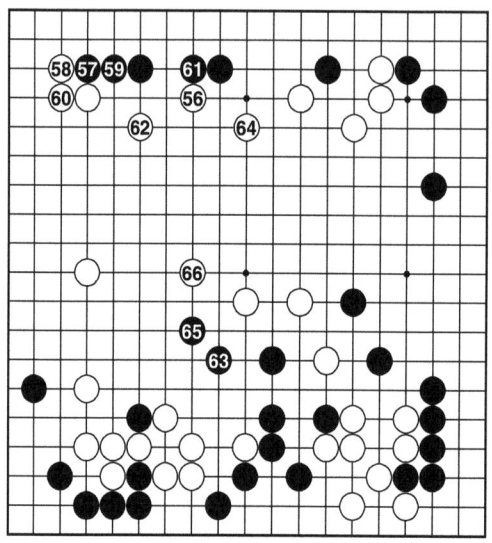

Figure 5 (56 – 66)

Figure 5

White can make a second moyo. This is my 'two-fold' large moyo.

While White has lost the moyo on the lower side, by shutting Black in with 56 to 62 he creates another moyo.

This illustrates the power of the large moyo strategy. Even if a moyo is invaded in one area, one can create another moyo elsewhere.

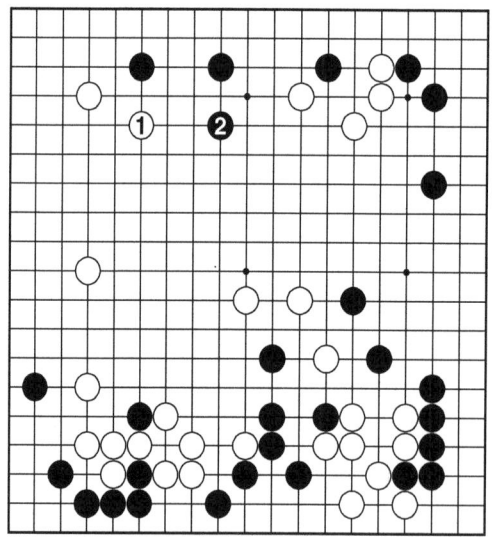

Dia. 8

Diagram 8

The keima 1 is in the right direction, but is just not good enough. Black easily moves into the White moyo with the tobi 2.

White 56 is a technique that is frequently used, and I advise you to remember it. It is a useful way of developing a moyo.

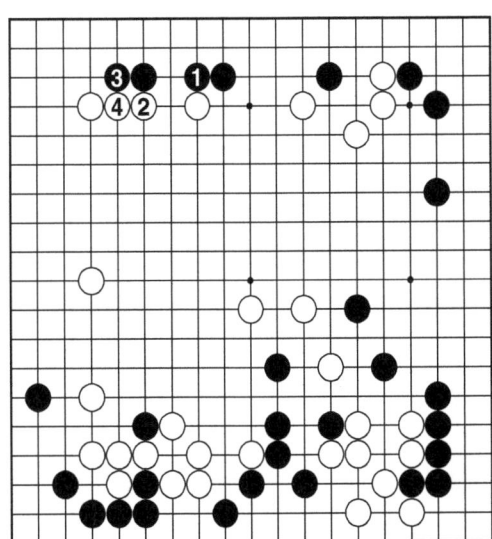

Dia. 9

Diagram 9

It is difficult to find a good answer to 56. If Black simply plays 1, White's tsuke at 2 constructs a solid wall.

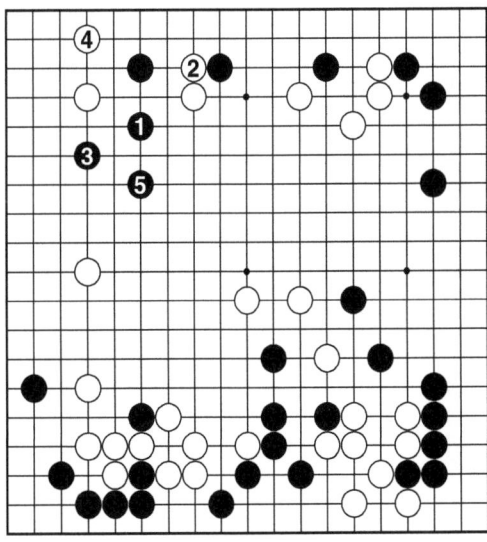

Dia. 10

Diagram 10

Of course, Black can play the tobi 1, but White's answer at 2 gains a large territory. Also, Black's group is not completely stable.

Black is in a difficult position.

After 57 to 60, Black took a long time to play 61. All these moves are not very natural; Black has problems.

With White 66, I was sure of winning.

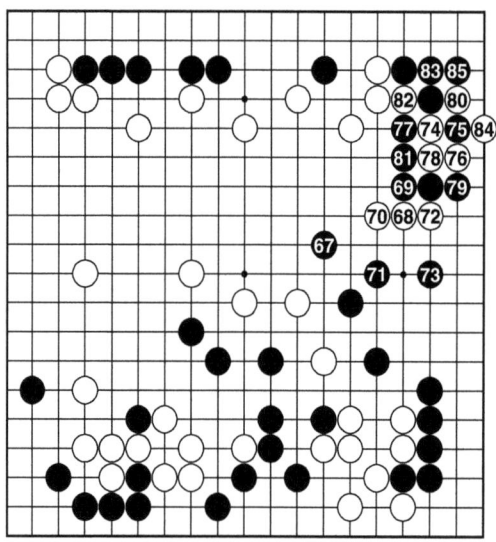

Figure 6 (67 – 85)

Figure 6

"Black 67 is the losing move", Mr Otake later told me. It is true that 68 is such a good move that Black does not have any good answer to it.

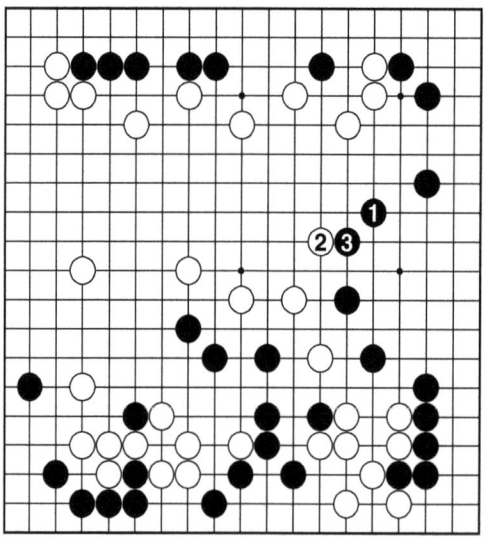

Dia. 11

Diagram 11

The keima 1 would have been better, as then White's kikashi cannot be placed any further than 2. Black has now closed off his territory on the side. I still think that White is in the lead, but perhaps this gives a closer game.

White 74 and 76 are decisive. I would prefer not to give a complicated commentary.

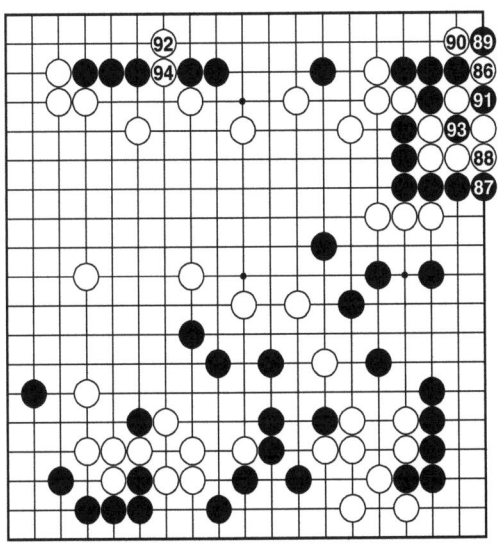

Figure 7 (86 – 94)

Figure 7

After 85 White starts a ko with 86. There was a superb ko threat for White at 92.

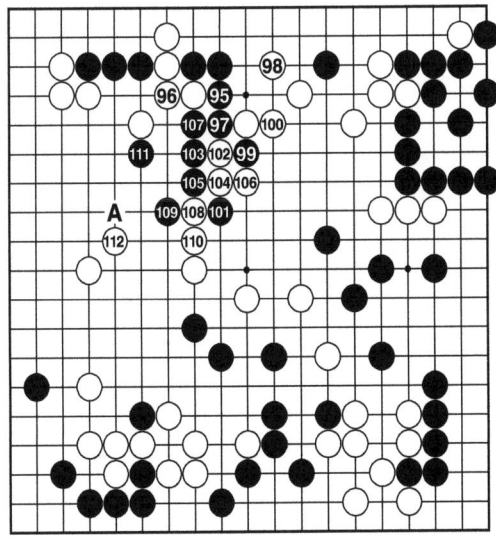

Figure 8 (95 – 112)

Figure 8

Black tries to start a fight with 95 and 97. White could kill Black, but by letting him live (if Black plays A his group is practically alive) I win calmly. Count territories to see that White is ahead.

White's first moyo disappeared, and so did the second. White even lets all of Black's groups live, but he still wins. A moyo is not only about making territory.

Result: In the end, White wins by 9½ points.

Chapter 4

Problems

I would first like to thank you for your attention so far. In this last chapter I give you eighteen problems based on the preceding material.

None of these problems are difficult. Whether it is a question of directing your stones towards the centre, playing the move that shines, seeing the goban clearly, or going beyond common sense, you will easily find the answer if you have followed the rest of this book.

Practically all of these problems are based on my games, so attentive readers already know the solutions. However, there may be better moves than those I played. You rarely get definitive answers in go. This is why one has to trust in one's intuition.

If you find an improvement on the solution I propose, then do please let me know.

Problem 1: Beware of common sense

Black to Play!

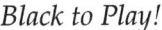

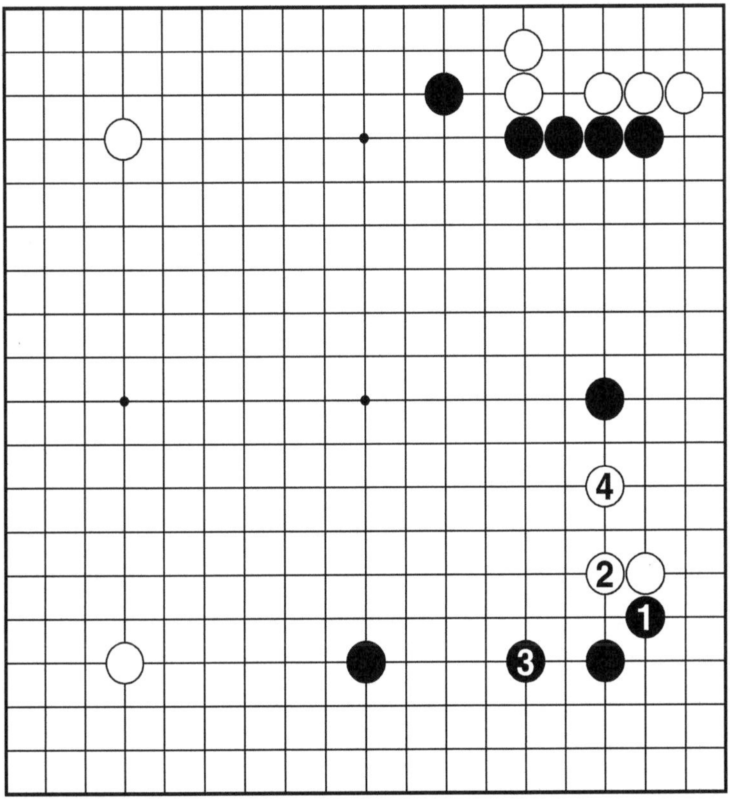

It is Black's move. Black has just played the standard attacking sequence 1 to 3. This sequence is to be found in many books. Strong players will know Black's answer to White 4, but is their common sense correct?

Doubting 'common sense' gives us another possibility.

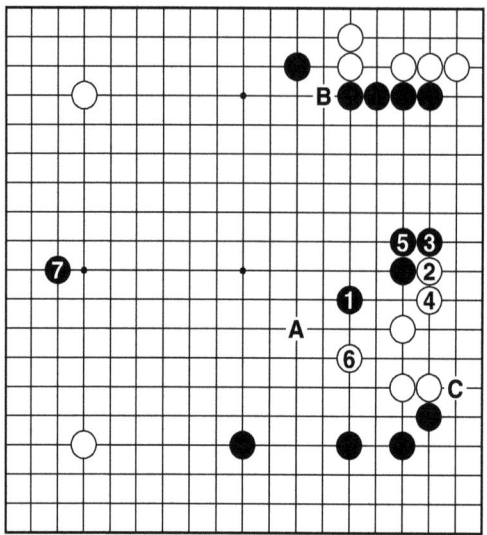

Problem 1: Solution

Solution
(the importance of the centre)

I propose the keima 1. Other reference books will say that 1 is bad as White easily settles his group with 2 and 4: they are wrong.

After 6, one can continue the attack on the White group with A, or one can play the wariuchi 7.

White's cut at B is less worrying since Black's centre has become more solid. Black can also continue the attack with the hane C.

Diagram 1
(the side is still open...)

The kosumi 1 is the standard attacking move. However, White can settle his group with 2 to 8. Black's side territory is still open, as White will play at A later on.

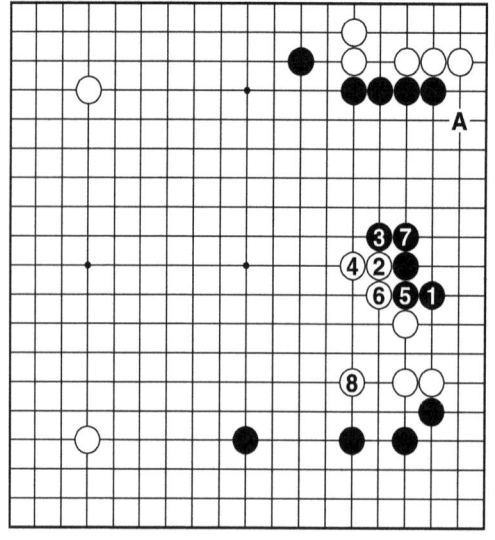

Dia. 1

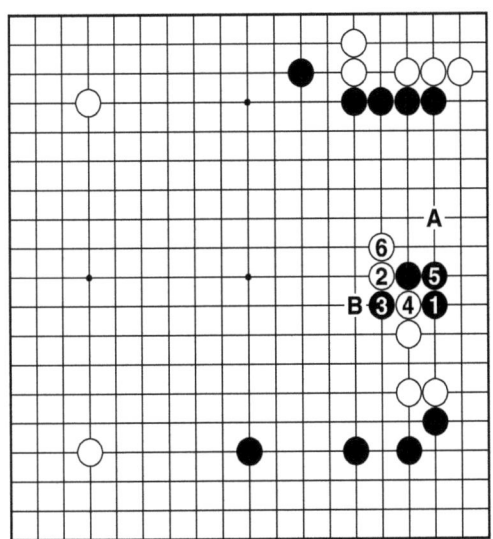

Dia. 2

Diagram 2
(dangerous for Black)

It is risky for Black to answer White 2 with 3 and 5. After White 6, the points A and B are miai.

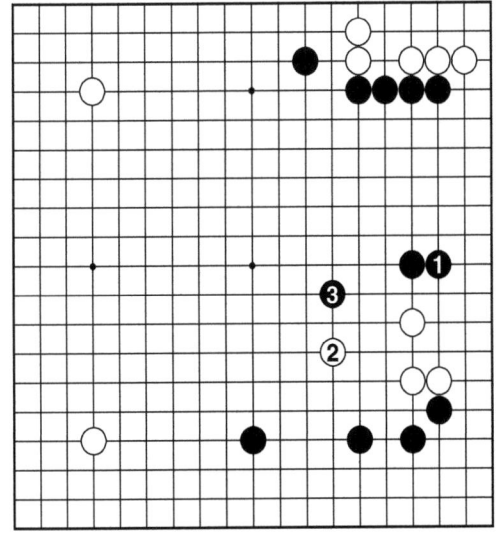

Dia. 3

Diagram 3

The best way to prevent White from settling the group is to play the tetchu 1. White can no longer play the tsuke (White 2 in Diagram 1).

However, this is less good for Black than my solution.

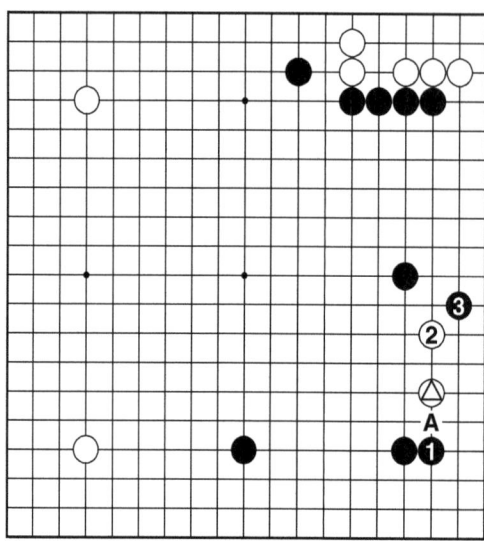

Dia. 4

**Diagram 4
(correct shape)**

While on this subject, here is another remark. The correct shape is to play the sagari 1 when White plays the kakari ⊘, rather than to play at A.

After 2, Black 3 prevents White from settling. I prefer this way of attacking to the way given in the problem Diagram.

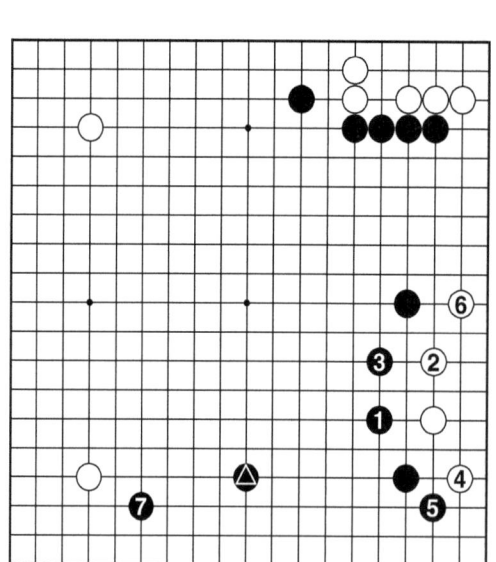

Dia. 5

**Diagram 5
(my advice)**

For some books, the boshi at 1 is taboo. However, after White lives underneath Black's stones Black gets to play the kakari 7, a move with great potential. Now the ● stone really shines.

Problem 2: The move that shines

White to Play!

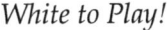

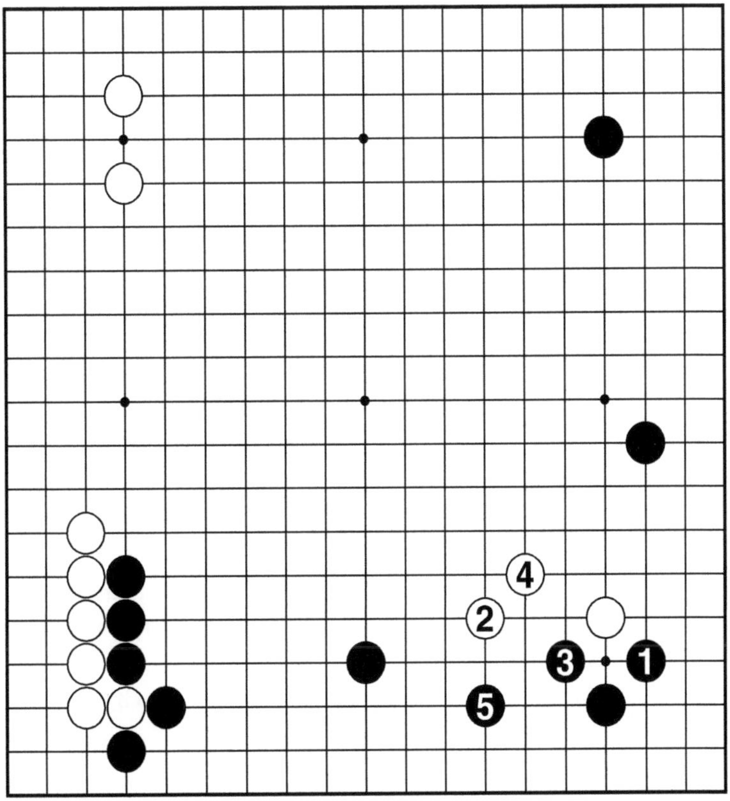

When Black plays 1, White aims to make a light, flexible shape (sabaki) with 2 and 4. The three white stones must not come under attack. With this guiding principle, find the move that shines. Of course, it is a question of direction.

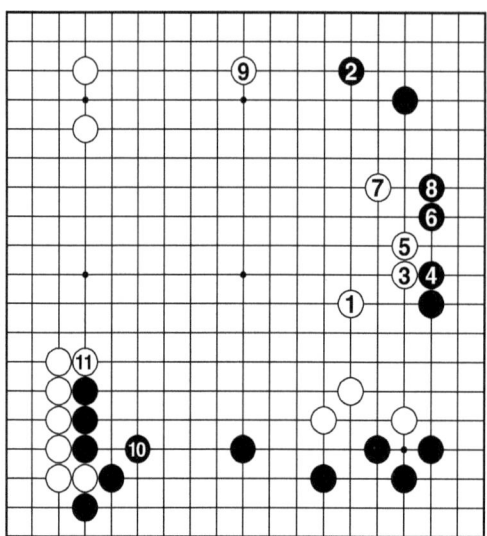

Problem 2: Solution

Solution
(central power)

White 1 is the key move.

Black can make a shimari with 2, but now White has an excellent follow-up: the kata-tsuke 3.

White plays the kikashi 3, 5 and 7, extends along the side with 9 and then plays the magari 11. Do you see how each of White's stones shines towards the centre?

Rather than worrying about the territory Black has gained (hardly any!), focus instead on White's central influence.

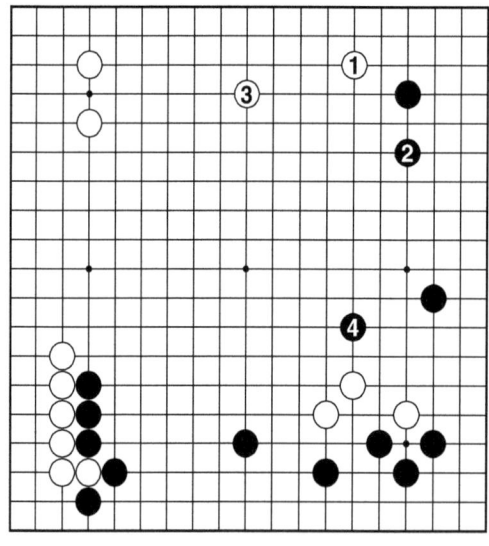

Dia. 1

Diagram 1
(the key move)

If you try to make territory, Black will play the key move 4.

Black's attack is more than enough compensation for White's territory.

Problem 3: The direction of the attack

Black to Play!

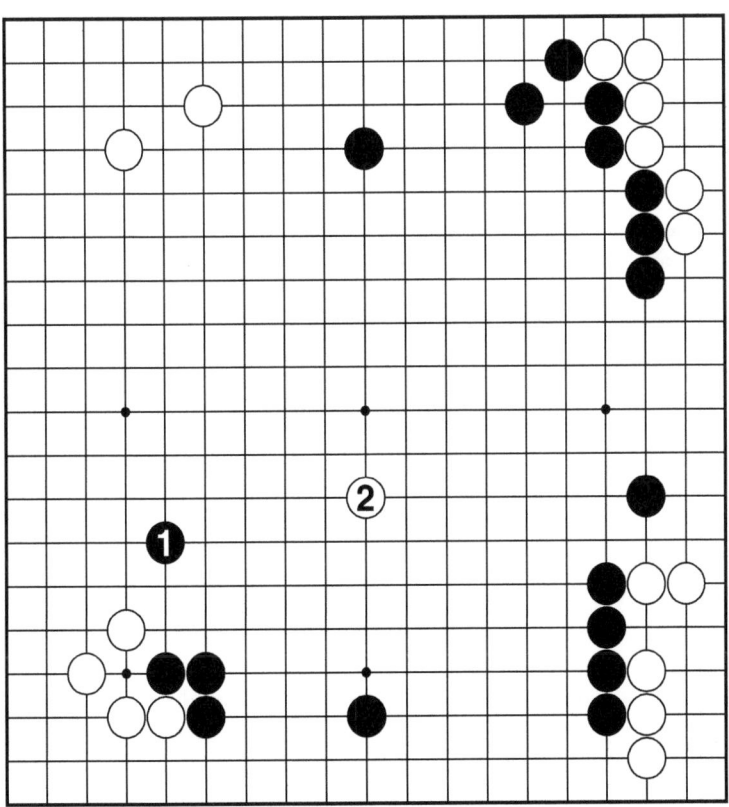

Perhaps 1 is a little grandiose, but I thought it would work well. Now, how should one deal with White's invasion at 2? This problem tests your feel for the game.

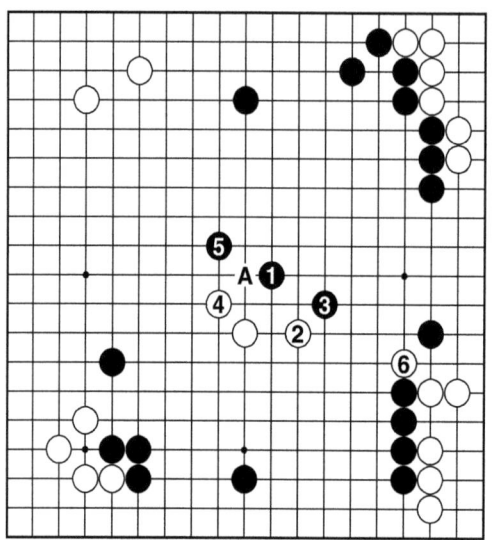

Problem 3: Solution

Solution
(the move I am proud of)

Here is a remark I often hear: "I like large-moyo games, but I often don't win them."

There are two possible reasons for losing a large-moyo game.

Firstly, you may believe that the purpose of a moyo is to make territory. This leads to trying too hard to make territory when your opponent invades. You may gain some, but it will not be enough.

The second reason is that you may make directional errors. You must be able to mount a good attack on any stone that invades your moyo. All is lost if your opponent makes sabaki and settles a group in your moyo.

If you choose the direction of your attack carefully, then even if your opponent succeeds in stabilising the invading stone, there will still be other possibilities open to you. For example, I am proud of Black 1. I believe this move results from the clear, unbiased way I see the goban.

After White 2, Black continues the attack with 3, and then again with 5. Black has built a new moyo above the stones 1, 3 and 5.

White has been aiming to play 6. One of the reasons for playing 1, instead of A, is Black's weakness at 6.

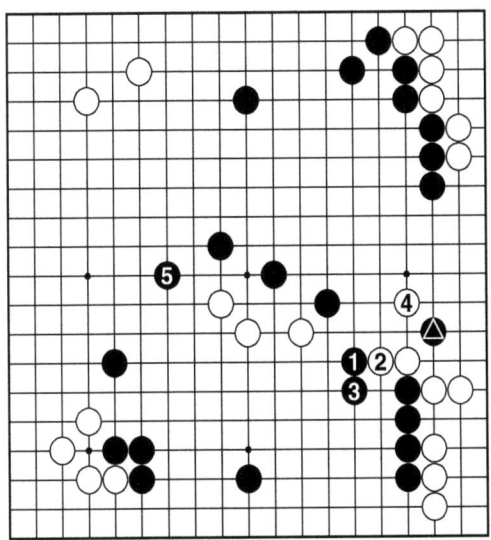

Dia. 1

Diagram 1
(simply sacrifice)

Black is aiming towards the centre, so the stone ⬣ is not important. Despite the points it lets White make with 2 and 4, Black 1 is an excellent move.

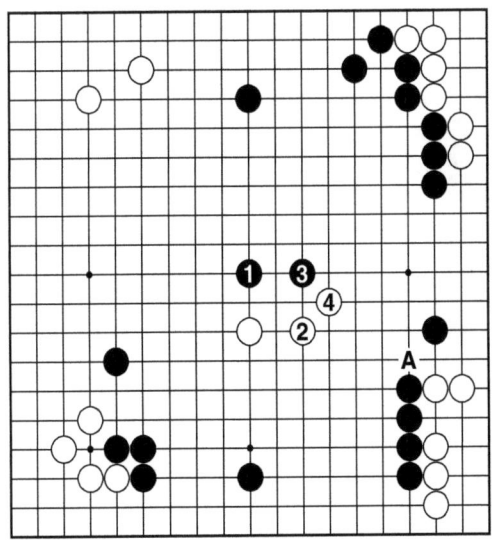

Diag. 2

Diagram 2
(good enough answer)

Black 1 is played in the right direction, but after 2 and 4 White will make good use of the weakness at A. This is less solid than the solution, and not quite as good.

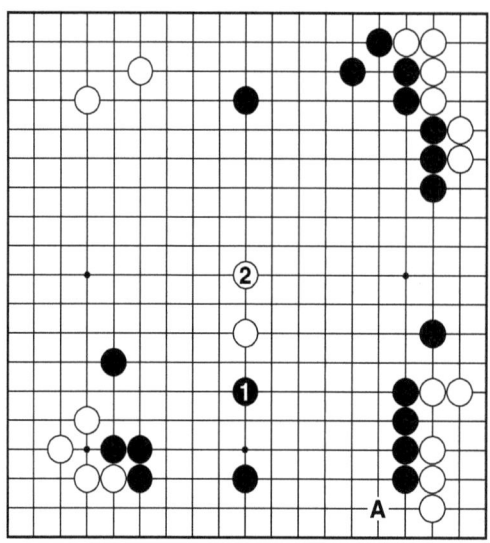

Dia. 3

Diagram 3
(wrong direction)

The worst idea is to make territory with 1. Black's central moyo is considerably diminished by White's tobi 2, and the lower side is still not entirely transformed into territory (White still has the tobi A).

This is a typical example of greed leading to a directional error.

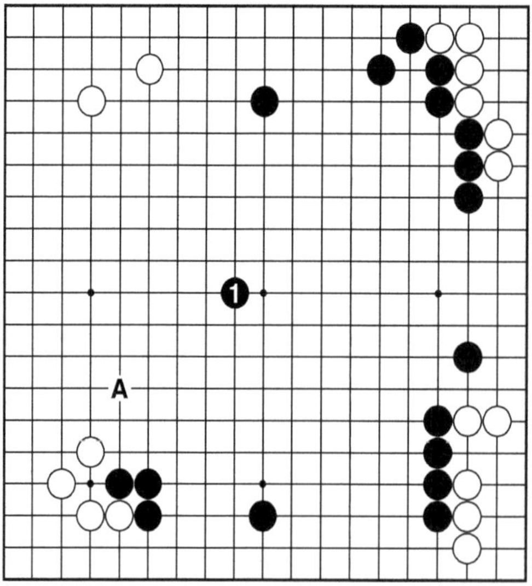

Diagram 4

Instead of playing at A, Black could have played the more standard move at 1.

But as you know, I cannot ever play the 'standard' move.

Dia. 4

Problem 4: A calm feeling

White to Play!

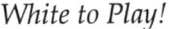

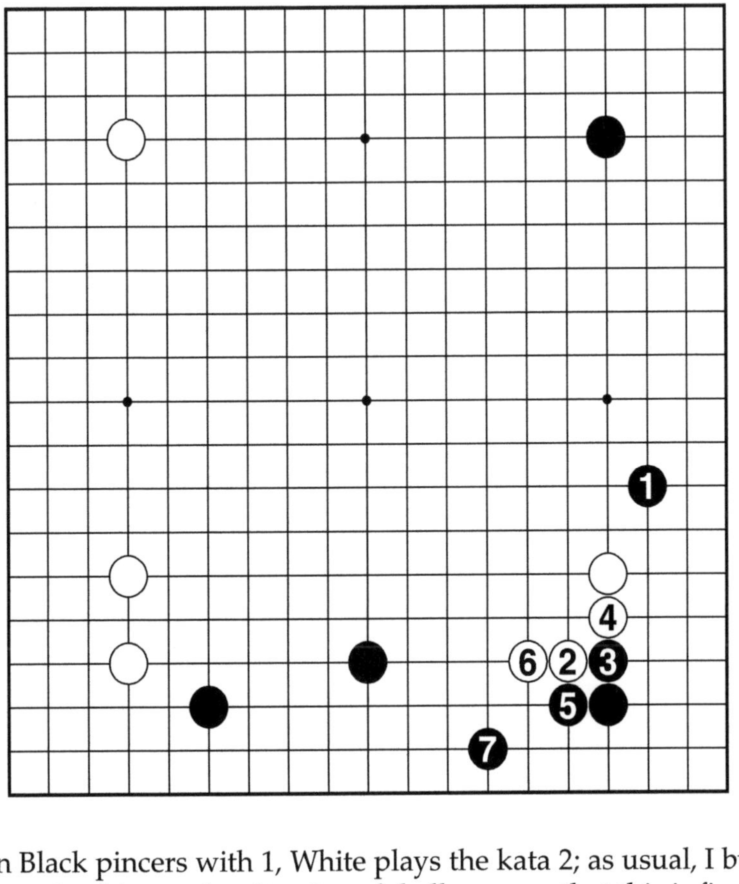

When Black pincers with 1, White plays the kata 2; as usual, I build influence. Looking at the situation globally we see that this is fine for White, as Black is forced to play low moves.

Now find White's next move. There are many big points on the goban, but there is no need to be in a hurry. With the cosmic style, it is important to take your time.

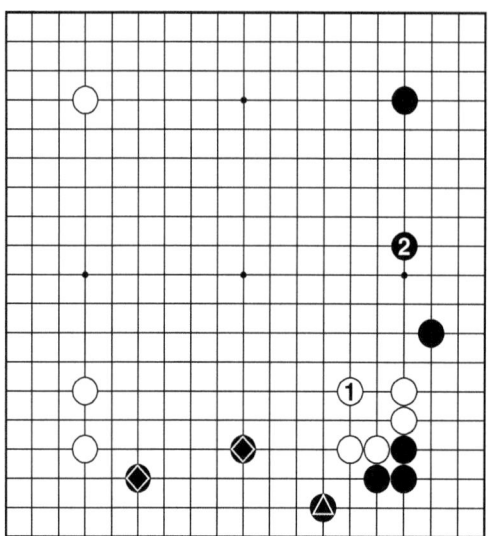

Problem 4: Solution

Solution

The correct response is White 1; White 1 is a honte (proper) move. If White wants to influence the centre, this group needs reinforcing.

By the way, note that as Black has played the suberi ▲, the two ◆ stones do not function very well.

Some may find this development good for Black, as Black makes a lot of territory. However, looking at the way the stones are working, I feel that it's good for White.

Diagram 1

One can attack Black's stone with 1, but I do not like this move, as I find it makes the game overly complicated.

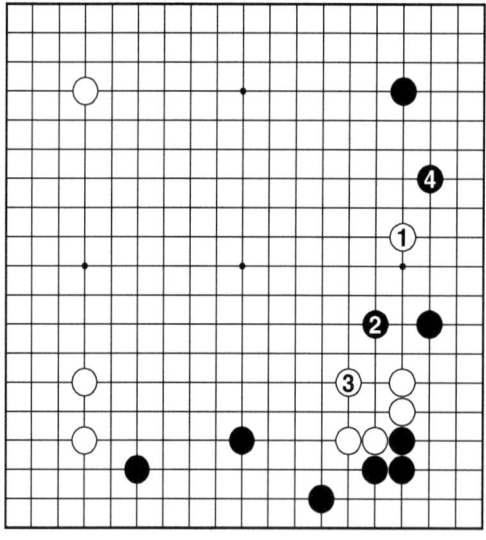

Dia. 1

Problem 5: It is best to play simply

White to Play!

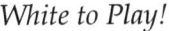

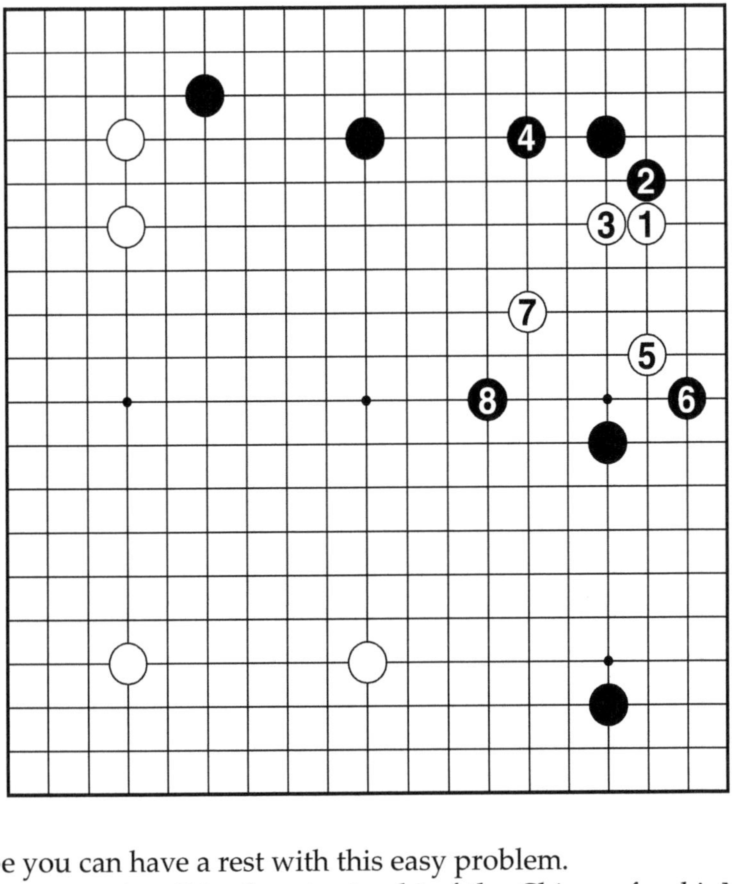

I hope you can have a rest with this easy problem.

The sequence 1 to 7 is almost a joseki of the Chinese fuseki. Next, Black aims to continue the attack with 8.

Let me give you a little hint for the next move: it is best to play simply.

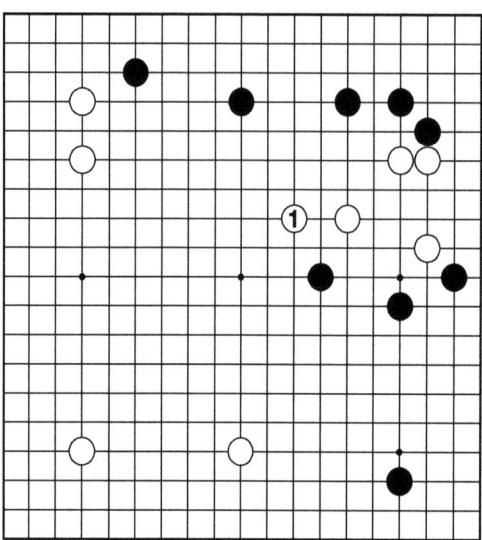

Solution
(the tobi)

I appreciate the beauty in stones, such as this tobi 1, that are directed towards the centre.

Before anything else is possible, White's group needs to get out into the open.

Problem 5: Solution

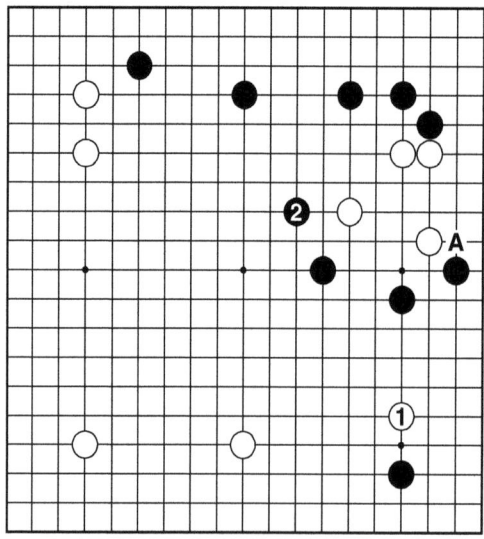

Diagram 1
(surrounded)

It is wrong to be too concerned with territory, as with White 1 here. Black would immediately play a capping move (boshi) at 1. White's group can still live with a move at A, but it is unacceptable to be closed in, and to have to live on such a small scale.

Dia. 1

Problem 6: The centre or the side?

Black to Play!

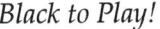

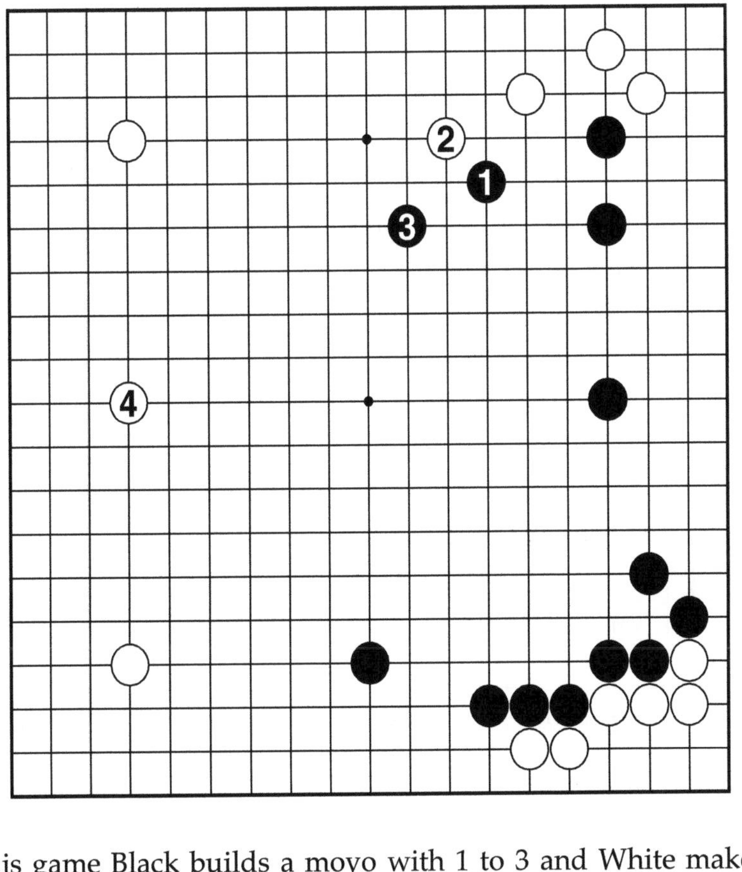

In this game Black builds a moyo with 1 to 3 and White makes a sanrensei with 4. Now, a very important choice for Black is whether to play in the centre, or to play on the right-hand side, which is still open.

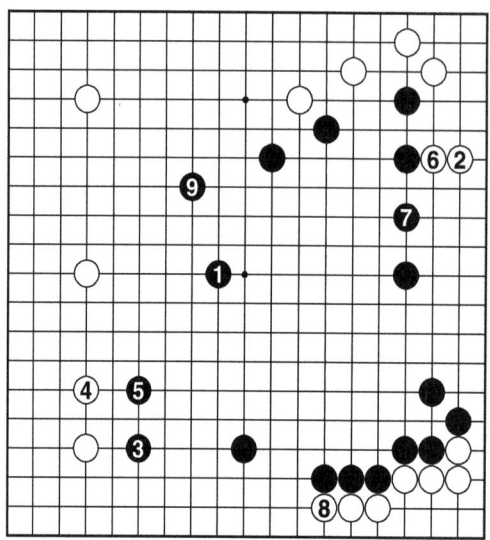

Problem 6: Solution

Solution (the centre)

All of Black's stones are ready to make a moyo in the centre. Black just needs to continue with this plan.

Black 1 seems to be the right point. White's suberi at 2 is not at all bothersome. Black develops the central moyo to its limit with 3 and 5; it has almost become secure territory.

Dia. 1

Diagram 1 (crippled moyo)

How cowardly you are if you play at 1! I hope you're satisfied with your tiny territory on the side. This petty way of playing lets White strike a deadly blow to your moyo with 2.

Problem 7: Compensation for territory

White to Play!

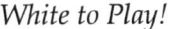

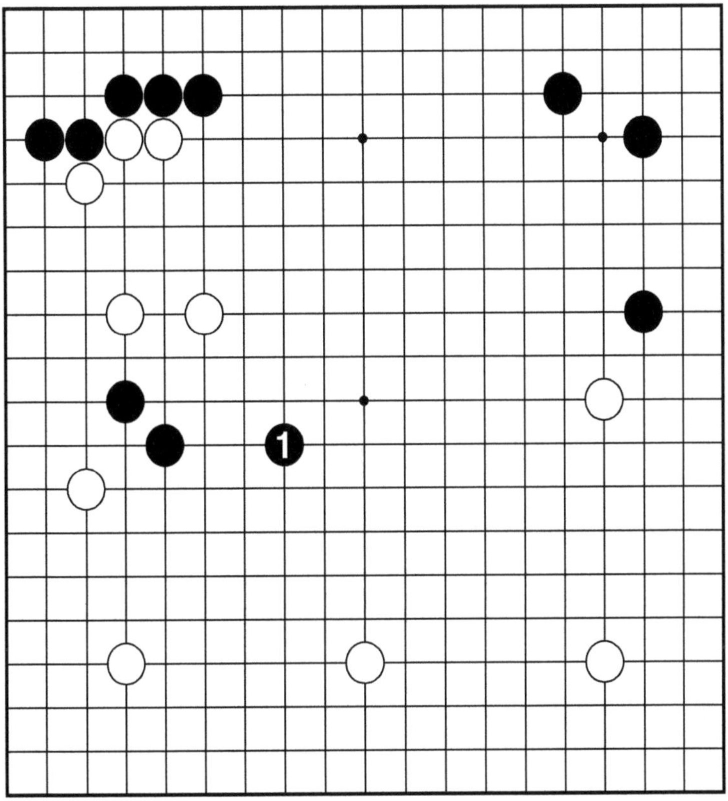

Black has just moved out into the centre with 1. While Black has gained territory little by little, White does not have any secure points. However, White is strong in the centre.

What should White seek in compensation for Black's territory?

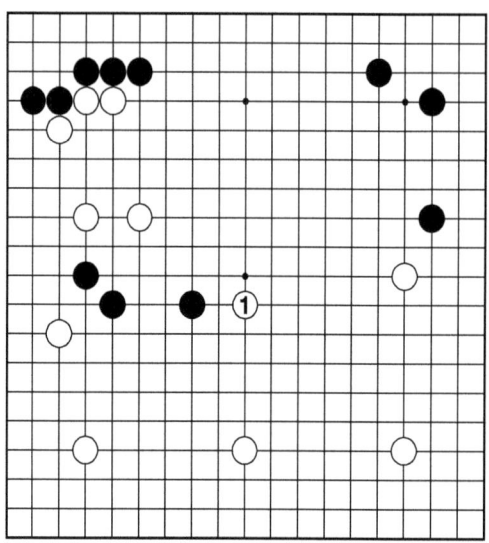

Solution
(the cap)

Of course, White should cap the third Black stone with 1. The sanrensei then comes into its own. This moyo is sufficient compensation for Black's territory.

Problem 7: Solution

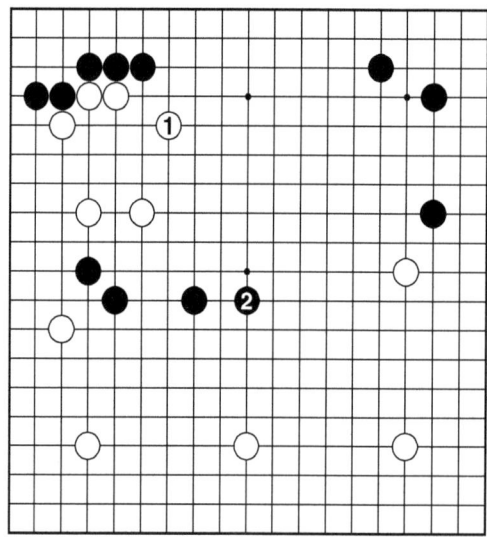

Diagram 1
(out of question)

White 1, say, is completely out of the question. Black plays the tobi 2, and White can no longer hope to mount an effective attack on this group. Also, the white stones on the lower side are now very weak.

Dia. 1

Problem 8: The tempting bad move

Black to Play!

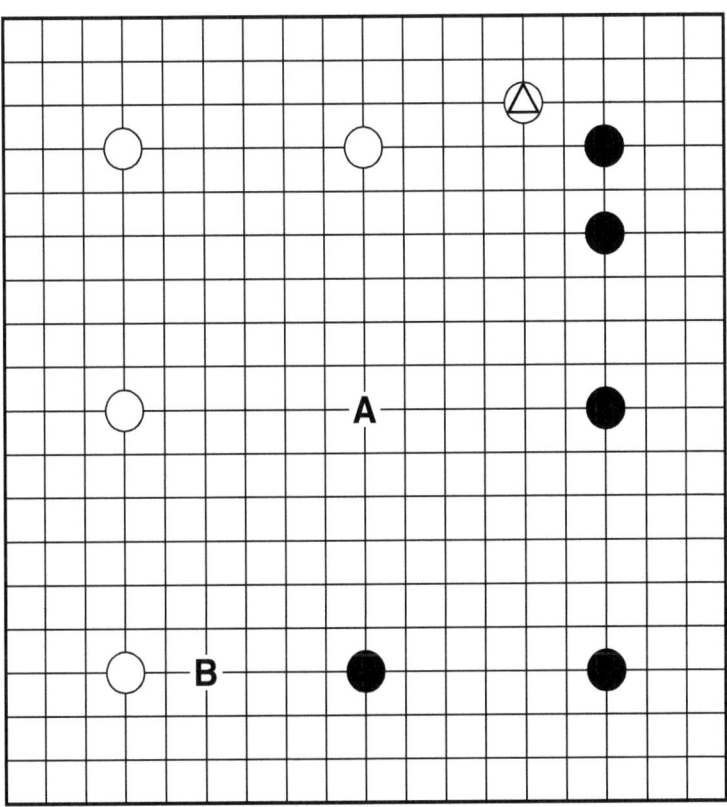

Normally, the cosmic style would suggest a move at A or B. However, I did not choose either of these moves. To turn the stone △ into a bad move, I decided to take the cosmic style on a risky adventure.

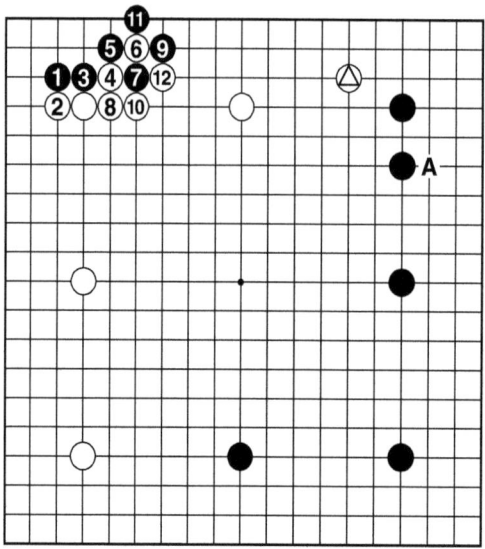

Problem 8: Solution

13 at 6

Solution
(the san-san)

Even with the cosmic style, I still played at the san-san, but not to make territory. I imagined the sequence up to 13. The stone ⊘ is then badly placed – it is as if the sequence had first been played and then White had played the kakari ⊘, on the wrong side (after the sequence, the kakari at A would be better).

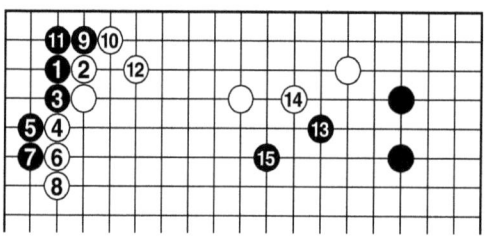

Dia. 1

Diagram 1
(two very good moves)

White can block on the other side with 2, but after 12, Black has two very good moves at 13 and 15.

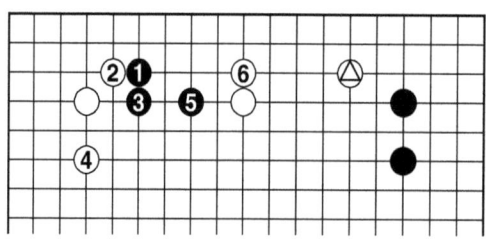

Dia. 2

Diagram 2
(unsatisfactory)

Black 1 provokes the sequence up to 6. Here we see that the ⊘ stone is well placed.

Problem 9: Even with your eyes closed...

White to Play!

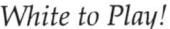

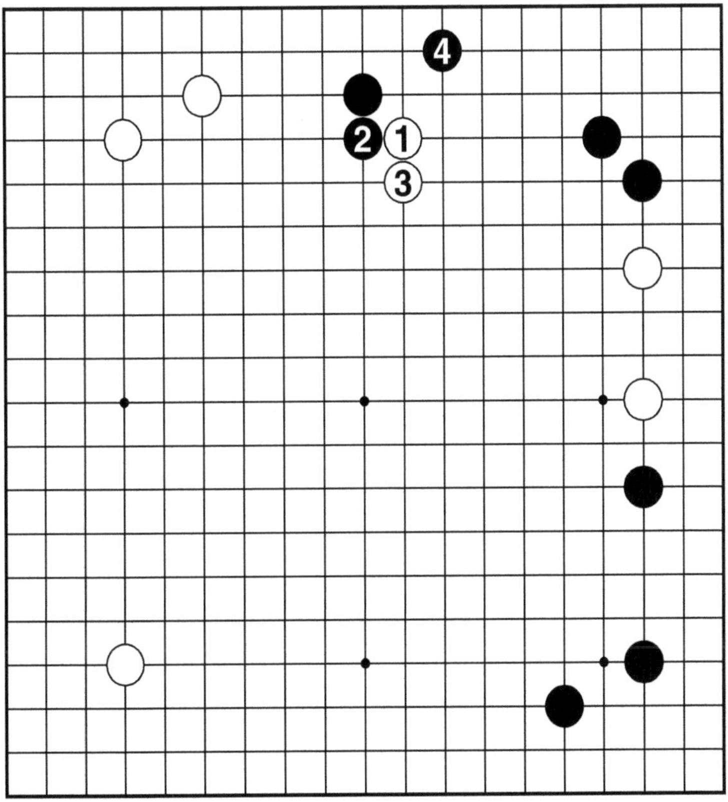

I did not play the kata-tsuke 1 to reduce Black's moyo, but rather to gain influence. I am sure you know what White must do next. Even with your eyes closed, you should be able to find the solution.

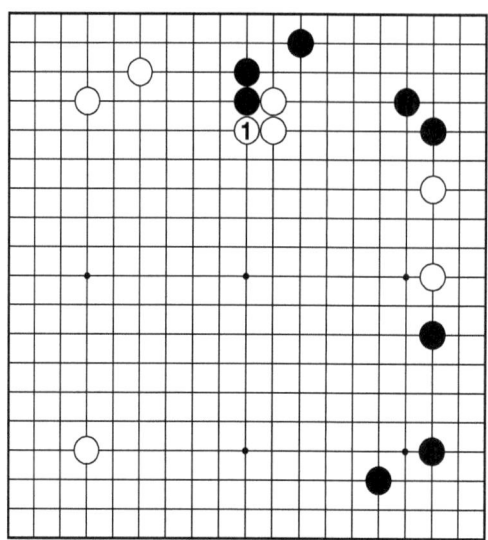

Solution
(thousand-ryo[1] magari)

The magari 1 is the only move I can imagine. White takes the initiative in the centre with this move. It really is a 'thousand-ryo' magari.

Problem 9: Solution

Diagram 1
(out of question)

White 1 is a big point, but it is out of the question. Black moves out towards the centre with 2 and 4, and now it is hard to see why the stone ⊘ was played at all.

Dia. 1

[1] *The ryo is an ancient Japanese currency. The term 'rhousand-ryo magari' refers to a vital move, decisive for the outcome of the game (Translator's note).*

Problem 10: The intuitive move

Black to Play!

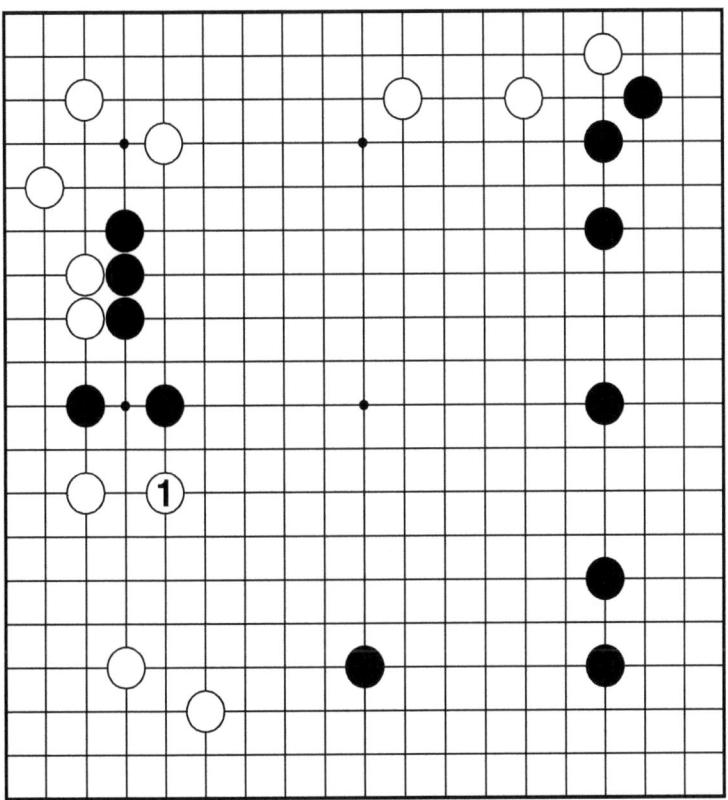

Black is trying to develop a moyo based on a sanrensei in this game. It is very difficult to decide on the next move. Even professionals have different opinions on this question.

Try to use your intuition.

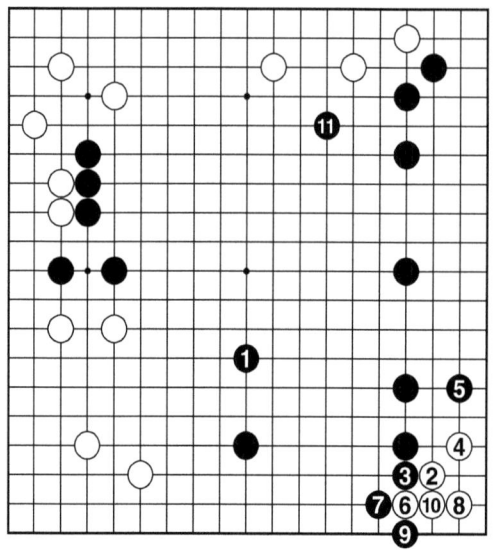

Problem 10: Solution

Solution
(the natural move)

Black is developing the right side and the centre, so I believe that 1 is natural.

Even if White invades the corner with 2 to 10, Black still gets to take sente and can play at 11. Black can now hope for a central moyo.

Dia. 1

Diagram 1
(small)

Black 1 is the correct move for reinforcing the corner. However, Black's moyo is wiped out by White 2. My intuition tells me to reject this idea.

The worst choice for Black 1 is the invasion at A. White B, Black C and White D then follow, and White moves easily into Black's moyo. Black A is a jealous move.

Problem 11: How to use thickness

Black to Play!

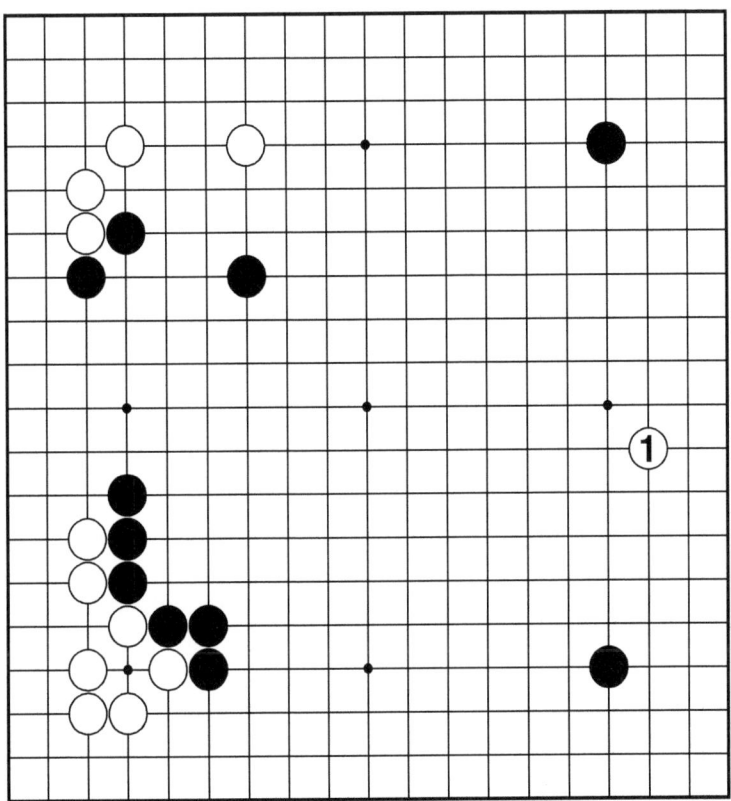

The theme of this problem is Black's central thickness. When White plays the wariuchi 1, how should Black play so as to make the most of this central power?

One which side of the stone 1 should one play a pincer? Or, is there another option?

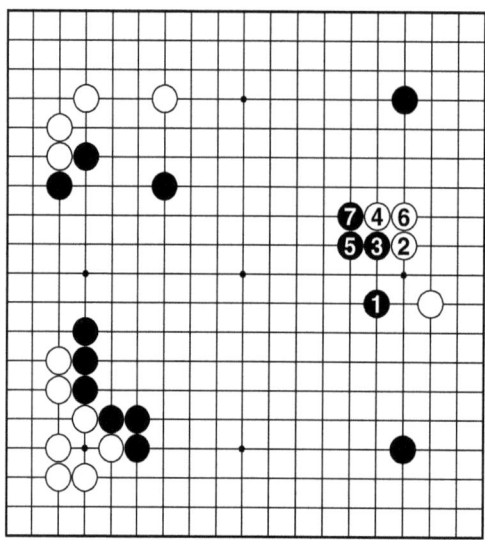

Problem 11: Solution

Solution
(the cap)

Black 1 is perfect for utilising Black's central thickness. If you feel this way then do play this move, without worrying about books that affirm that fuseki plays should be on the third or fourth lines.

After White's answer at 2 and the sequence 3 to 7, the centre has been painted black.

Dia. 1

Diagram 1
(a bad exchange)

Generally the exchange of 1 for 2 is fine for Black. However in this position it is unsatisfactory, as the tobi 2 reduces Black's central moyo.

The common-sense move is, again, just not good enough.

Problem 12: The tennôzan

White to Play!

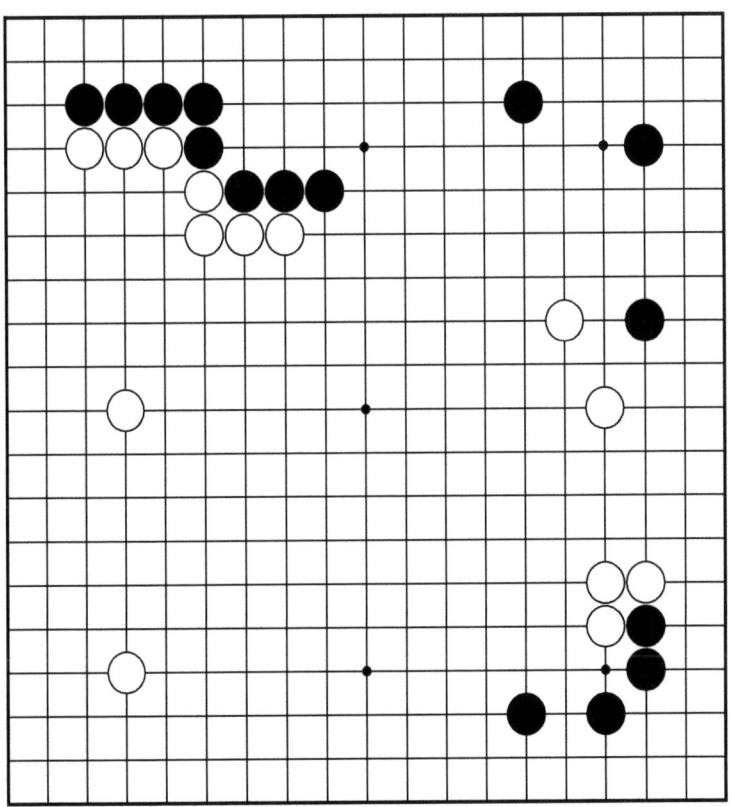

This is purely and simply a question of the tennôzan. Even kyu players can find the solution, if they have a clear vision of the goban.

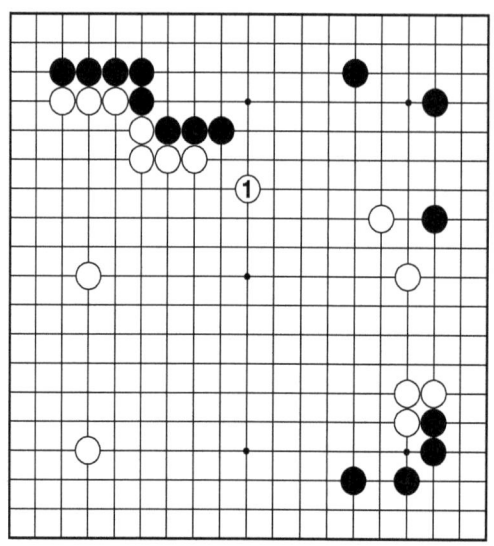

Solution
(double keima)

I call White 1 on the tennôzan a 'double keima', as with one move White's moyo is developed, and Black's moyo is reduced.

White really gets two moves for the price of one.

Problem 12: Solution

Diagram 1
(too local)

White 1 just develops the left side and is too local. White's moyo on the left side is limited by Black's good move at 2.

Dia. 2

Problem 13: How to deal with an invasion

Black to Play!

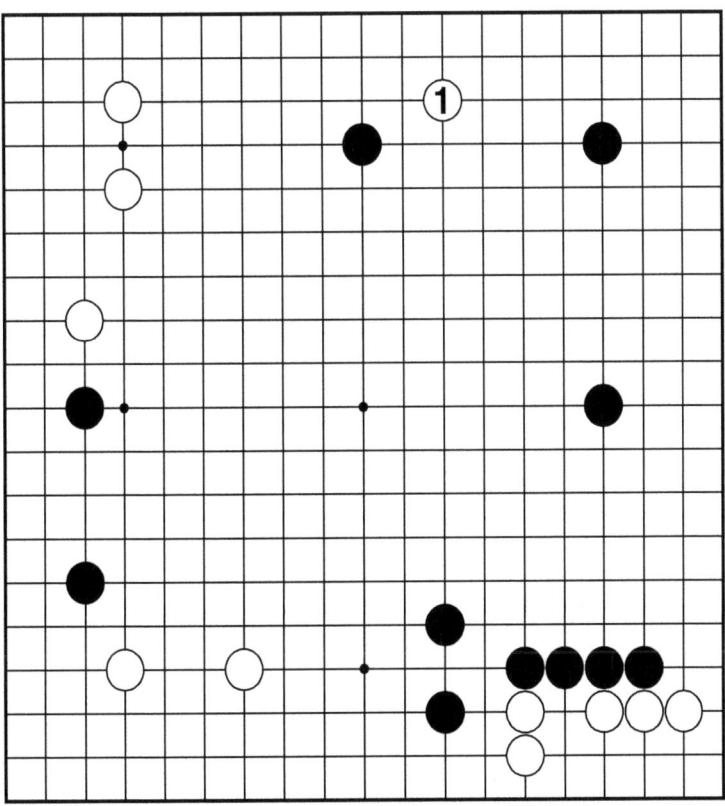

White has just invaded at 1. Black can now either attack this stone, or build central influence. The answer is one of these two options. Find the move that is adapted to the global situation.

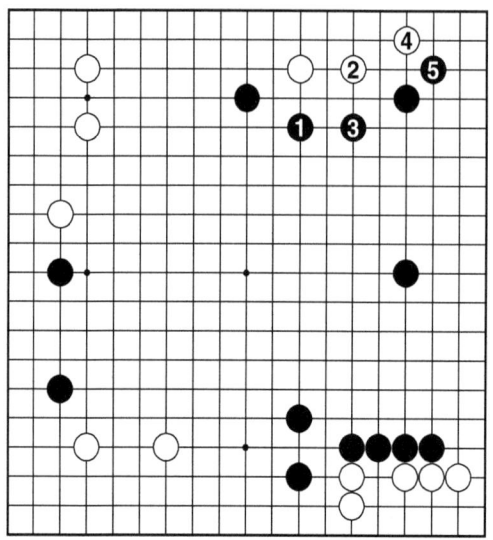

Problem 13: Solution

Solution
(the centre is very big)

In line with intuition, the boshi 1 is very attractive. White settles the invading group with 2 and 4, but Black walls the group in with 1 and 3, and is extremely happy to see a moyo develop on the right side.

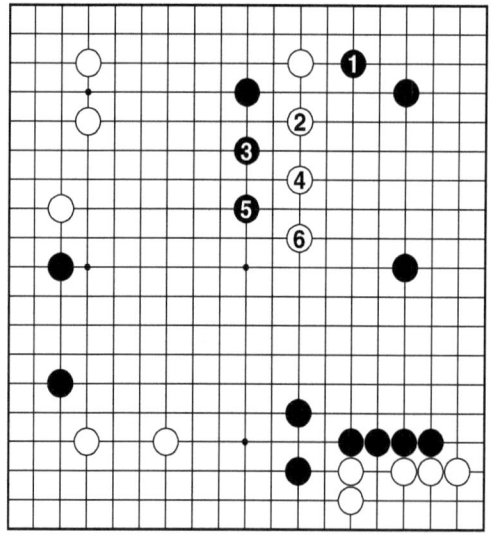

Dia. 1

Diagram 1
(unfavourable tobi)

Black plays 1 to attack White's stone. However, the three tobi of 2, 4 and 6 destroy Black's moyo. This is not good for Black.

Problem 14: I want to play this move

White to Play!

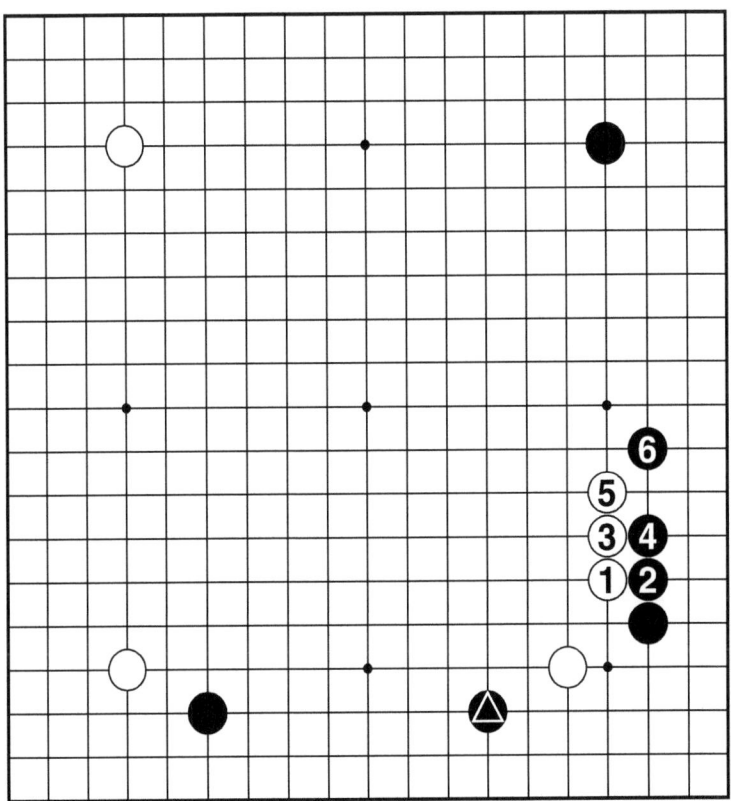

I played the kake 1 in answer to the pincer stone ⬣. You have probably never seen a move like this. I decided to play this way as I knew what I wanted to play next...

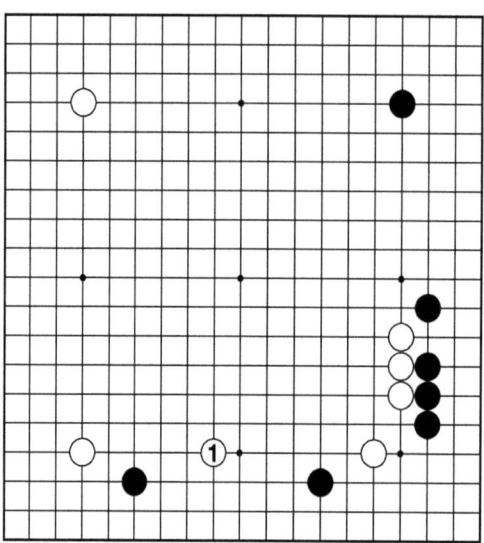

**Solution
(attack)**

White gains an attack on the two black stones in compensation for the territory Black has just made. White takes the initiative with 1. Now White takes the lead, as long as White prevents Black's stones from settling too easily.

Problem 14: Solution

**Diagram 1
(too calm)**

Although I am easy-going, I do find White 1 to be too slow. What can White hope for, in compensation for Black's territory, after Black plays 2?

Dia. 1

Problem 15: The leaning attack

Black to Play!

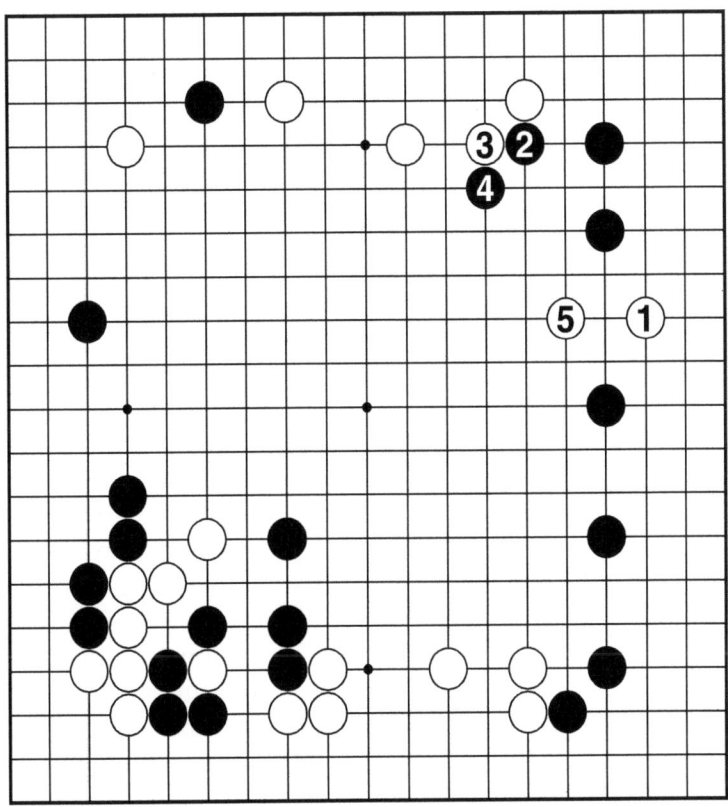

The leaning attack of 2 and 4 on the invading stone 1 is a common technique. Now think about Black's answer to White's tobi 5. This is a difficult problem, but here is a hint: try to find a move that prepares the attack.

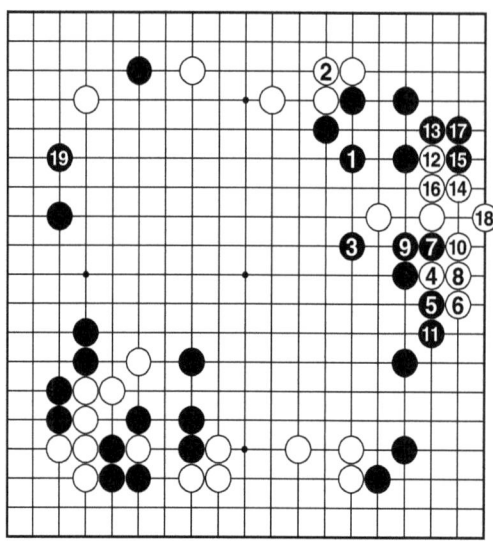

Problem 15: Solution

Solution
(the kaketsugi I am proud of)

I am really proud of this kaketsugi.

When White connects at 2, the kake 3 is the idea behind the kaketsugi. Then White lives with difficulty, and Black gets to take the last big point at 19. Black is now in the lead.

Diagram 1
(the standard move...)

There is nothing wrong with taking territory with 1 and 3; in fact most professionals would play in this manner. However I am not happy to let the stones ⬠ escape, even if I do gain some territory. I do not like this result at all.

Dia. 1

Problem 16: Continue with your idea

Black to Play!

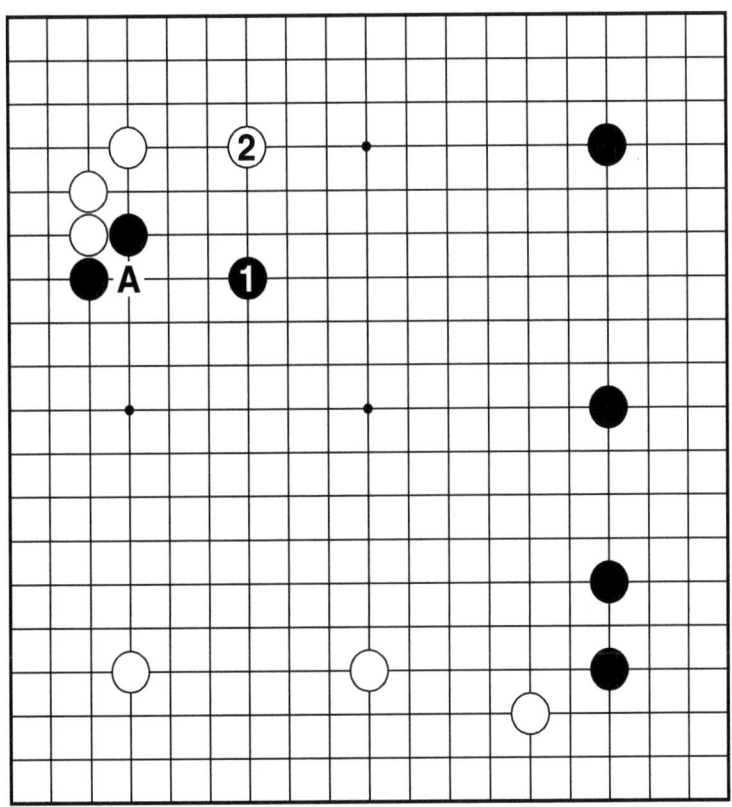

Instead of connecting at A, I played the ogeima 1 to move out into the centre as quickly as possible. Next, how can Black develop this idea?

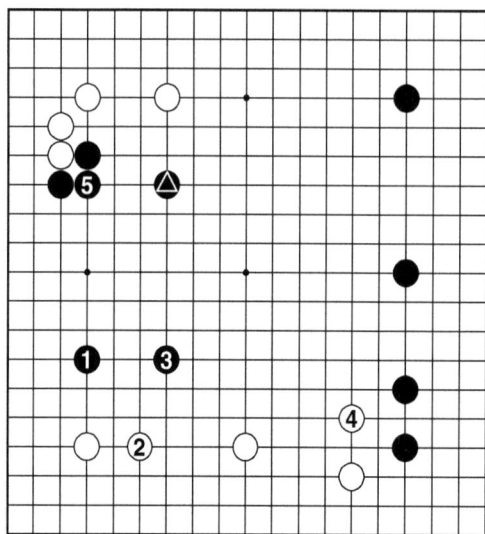

Problem 16: Solution

Solution
(towards the centre)

I played the kakari 1, and then the tobi 3, moving towards the centre. Even now, I do not know if these are the best moves, but I hope you can sense how well these moves work with the stone ⬤.

Black 5 creates a large moyo, stretching from the side to the centre. Of course, I am happy with this result.

Diagram 1
(inconsistent)

As the ⬤ stone is not there to make territory, it is inconsistent to try to make territory with 1 and 3. Also, White 4 and 6 have become very good moves.

Dia. 1

Problem 17: Use your intuition

Black to Play!

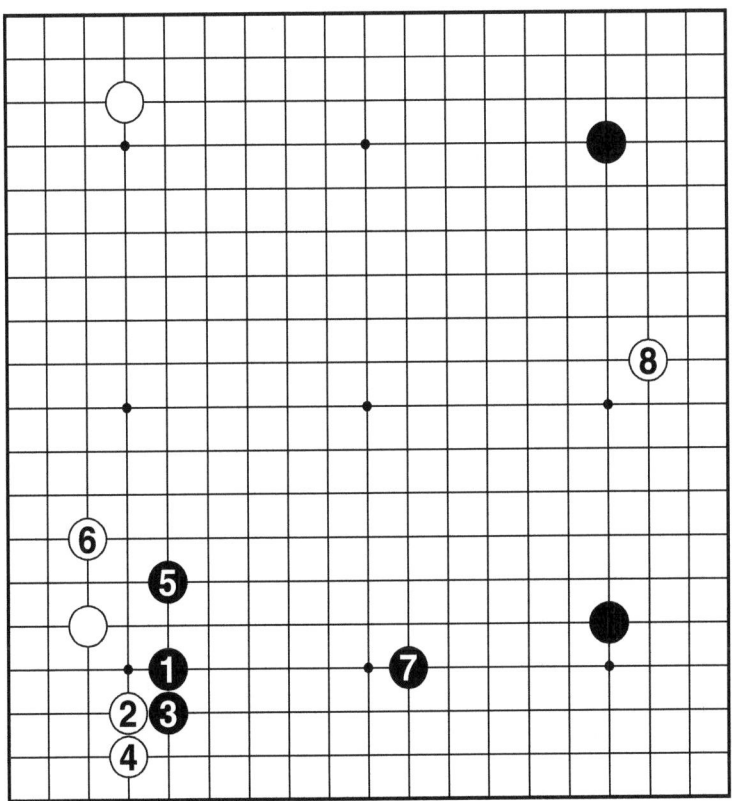

Clearly, Black has played the sequence 1 to 7 to create a moyo. Therefore Black cannot be satisfied with a 'normal' move after White 8. Use your intuition to find the next move.

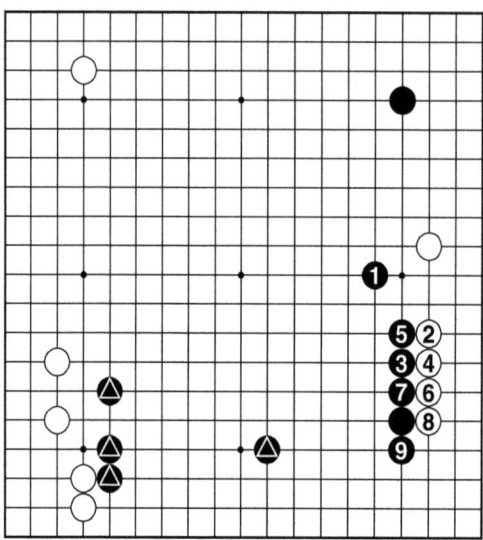

Problem 17: Solution

Solution
(the fifth line is the line of life)

Black 1 on the fifth line gives life to Black's game. Black answers the niken-baraki 2 with the kata-tsuke 3, an influence building move. These vigorous plays really make the four stones ⊘ shine.

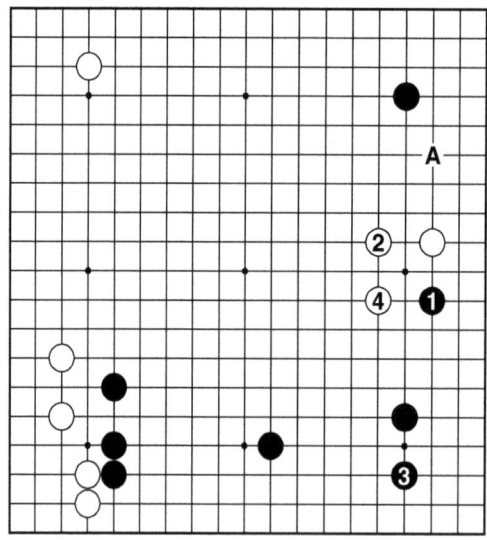

Dia. 1

Diagram 1
(a normal game)

White plays the tobi 2 instead of extending at A, after Black's extension at 1. Again, this is a move on the fifth line (the line of life). When Black makes a shimari with 3, we have a normal game. However, the cosmic style isn't about playing 'normal' games.

Problem 18: The movie I am proud of

White to Play!

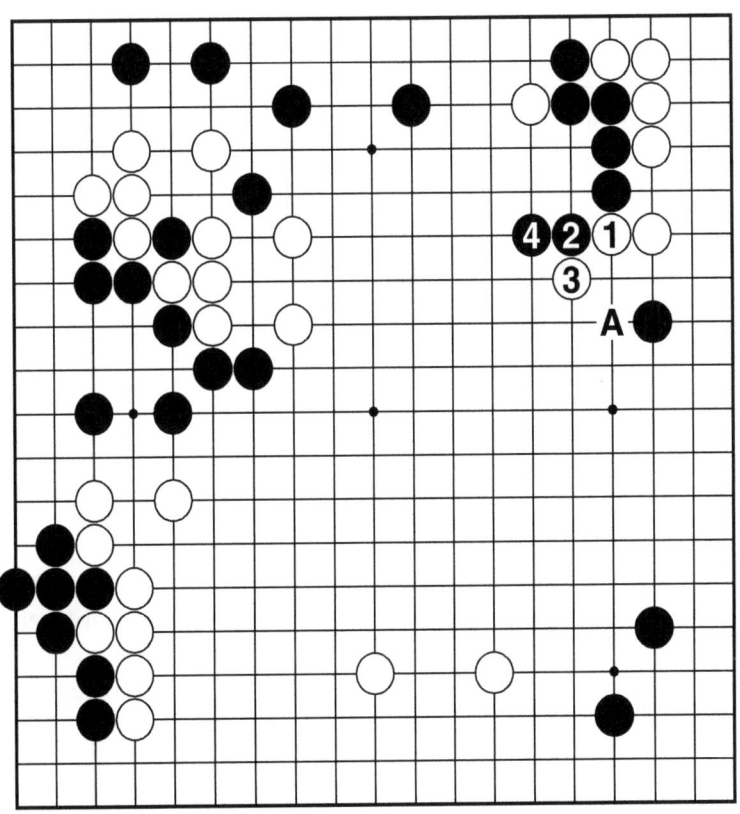

Here, finally, is the last problem.

The sequence 1 to 4 is very common. Now please do think carefully about the next move. The usual move at A is not good enough. I am really proud of the next move.

This problem is very difficult, so don't worry if you don't get it.

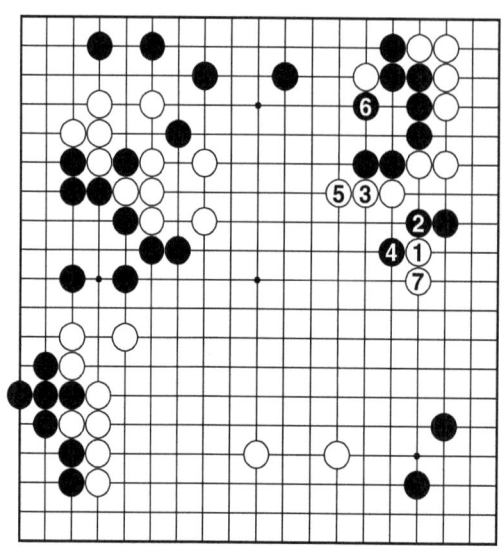

Solution (kake)

My solution is the kake 1. Of course, if Black resists with 2 and 4, White plays the kikashi 3 and 5, and then plays the nobi 7.

I felt that this fight wasn't promising for Black.

Problem 18: Solution

Diagram 1 (unsatisfactory)

The sequence 1 to 5 is normal, but the 3 and 5 stones are not effective towards the centre. Also Black has a sente move, the magari at A (A is sente because of the threat of Black B, White C and Black D).

I am very unhappy with this result.

Dia. 1

Takemiya Masaki

© *1995 Yasuo Tamura*

Takemiya Masaki was born on January 1st, 1951 in Tokyo. As a child he was a disciple of Minaichi Tanaka 7-dan. In 1961 he became a disciple of Kitani Minoru 9-dan and the same year entered the professional ranks as a 1-dan. In 1977 he attained the top rank of 9-dan.

He was known as one of Kitani's 'three musketeers' (the other two were Ishida Yoshio and Kato Masao). In 1968, at the age of 17, he came eighth in the Pro Juketsu tournament. The following year he came fifth in this tournament, thus earning the nickname 'Juketsu boy'.

In 1976 he took the Honinbo title. The next year he lost this title, but retook it in 1980, and held it again from 1985 to 1988. He has also won two international Fujitsu tournaments, along with the Judan and many other titles.

At present he is renowned throughout the world of go as the uncontested master of the sanrensei. His 'cosmic style', which seeks out the realm of dreams on the goban and emphasises intuition, is highly popular among all go players.

YAMADA SHINJI

HOW TO PLAY GO
THE **AI WAY**!

Explained with illustrative diagrams

This book is intended for amateurs in go who would like to learn and employ the modern AI style. The AI style may seem confusing because there are so many tactics far away from traditional thinking. But the study of the new techniques introduced by AI has already lead to their rapid spread and adoption. Today they are applied by pros almost as a matter of course.

This book summarizes the findings from the study of AI techniques and explains them with illustrative diagrams.

"I wrote this book with a lot of enthusiasm and I hope that this way everybody can profit from the insights of my studies. I am very happy to be able to witness this important turning point towards a new era, in which an AI can defeat humans in the game of go. Engaging with the AI style has given me joy like I have never felt before in go. I hope this kind of joy will be conveyed and passed on through the book." Yamada Shinji 6p

ISBN 978-3-940563-40-8

2020, 196 pages

BOARD N'STONES